COOKIES
GALORE

Sweet and smart: Susan Sarandon (at right) and her family are fans of the natural treats made by Bethenny (at left).

How to healthy-up cookies

Add ground flaxseeds (try 1 tablespoon) to batter for more fiber and omega-3 fatty acids.

Experiment with different natural, healthy sweeteners, like honey and agave syrup instead of the sugar. You can also try this in other recipes that call for plain granulated sugar.

Use this cookie base (minus the last 3 ingredients) as a blank canvas for other flavor variations. So instead of using bananas, walnuts, and chocolate chips, **try one of the following:**
- raisins and a pinch of cinnamon
- dried blueberries with raw sugar sprinkled on cookies
- dried cranberries and ½ teaspoon orange extract
- slivered almonds and ½ teaspoon almond extract

Banana-Oatmeal-Chocolate Chip Cookies

Prep: 10 Minutes
Cook: 25 minutes
Makes 16 cookies

1 cup oat flour
¾ cup old-fashioned rolled oats
½ teaspoon baking powder
⅓ teaspoon baking soda
½ teaspoon salt
½ cup raw sugar
⅓ cup canola oil
⅓ cup plain soy milk
½ teaspoon vanilla extract
½ ripe banana, cut into small pieces
¼ cup chopped walnuts or other favorite nut
⅓ cup semisweet vegan chocolate chips (such as Tropical Source)

1. Preheat oven to 350°. Combine first 6 ingredients (through sugar) in a bowl. Whisk together oil, soy milk, and vanilla in a separate bowl. Add wet mixture to dry ingredients; stir to combine. Fold in banana, walnuts, and chocolate chips.
2. Line a baking sheet with parchment paper. Scoop dough onto pan with a small ice-cream scoop. Bake 25 minutes or until golden brown, turning baking sheet halfway through. Let cool on a wire rack.

Calories 138; Fat 8g (sat 1g, mono 4g, poly 2g); Cholesterol 0mg; Protein 2g; Carbohydrate 16g; Sugars 9g; Fiber 1g; Iron 1mg; Sodium 114mg; Calcium 16mg ●

Find out more about Bethenny at www.bethennybakes.com.

MQP

An Hachette Livre Company

First published in Great Britain in 2006 by
MQ Publications, a division of Octopus
Publishing Group Ltd
2–4 Heron Quays
London E14 4JP

www.octopusbooks.co.uk

Photography: Marie Louise Avery
& Chris Alack see page 192
Design concept & layout: Clare Barber
Recipe credits: see page 192

ISBN 1-84072-997-X
ISBN 978-1-84072-997-9

2 3 4 5 6 7 8 9 10

Printed and bound in China

CONTENTS

INTRODUCTION

Nothing can beat the aroma of a freshly baked cookie. Homemade cookies make a wonderful gift to brighten someone's day and they are great fun to make with children.

★ ORIGINS ★

The word cookie has become commonplace all over the world but in Britain the word biscuit is also used. Cookie comes from the Dutch word *koekje* and it means little cake. Biscuit on the other hand comes from the French *bis cuit* and it means twice cooked. This harks back to the days when bakers put slices of fresh baked bread back in the oven to dry out and they became hard like rusks. This of course improved the keeping qualities, and was especially important when such foods were taken on long sea voyages and had to keep for a long length of time. Nowadays, soft cake-like confections are known as cookies (choc chip cookies for example) whereas crisper versions, such as shortbread are known as biscuits.

Apart from the obvious satisfaction which comes from making your own cookies, there is the added advantage that you can use the best ingredients and know exactly what they contain. Cookies are easy to make and many in this book are of the free-form kind, which you either spoon onto a tray or shape with your hands, so no extra equipment is needed. Homemade cookies are always popular so if you refrain from making them because they will all disappear in a flash, then make the refrigerator type where you slice off the raw dough as you need them or make sure you have some freezer bags handy to pop some in the deep freeze. Cookies are not only great as a midmorning treat, they are also good in lunchboxes and make a great quick dessert when accompanied by ice cream or thick fruity yogurt.

★ GET BAKING ★

There is something very therapeutic about baking cookies—it is to do with allowing ourselves to play again. Children love baking and you can have such fun with them, so don't just look at the wonderful pictures in this book—get baking and bring pleasure to yourself and those you love.

EQUIPMENT

To bake good cookies you don't need fancy equipment but here are a few tips on items you will need.

★ BOWLS ★

These can be of glass, ceramic, or stainless steel, it does not matter which, but what is important if you are using a hand-held electric mixer is that the bowl is tall and deep rather than wide and shallow. Sugar, flour, and especially confectioners' sugar tend to fly out of a shallow bowl.

★ HAND-HELD ELECTRIC MIXER ★

Although not absolutely necessary, a hand-held electric mixer is so handy and quick for creaming butter and sugar and for beating egg whites.

★ MEASURES ★

A set of measuring cups and spoons is vital for measuring quantities down to a fraction of a teaspoon. The amounts given in the recipes are for level cupfuls and spoonfuls unless stated otherwise. A set of scales is also desirable as cookies, like cakes, require accurate measuring of ingredients.

★ COOKIE SHEETS & BROWNIE PANS ★

Cookies can burn easily so it is wise to buy heavy professional quality sheets and pans. Every pan will bake a little differently depending on the weight, thickness, and material it's made from. Lining with parchment paper helps promote even baking as does placing a thin cookie sheet or brownie pan on top of another cookie sheet for extra insulation. Baking sheets should be rimless or with low rims so that it is easy to remove the cookies. Air-cushioned baking sheets bake evenly but they may take a little longer and generally are better when you want to end up with soft chewy cookies rather than crisp ones.

★ TIMER ★

Timing is vital—cookies are easily overcooked if left a few minutes too long, so a timer with a loud ring will keep you alerted.

★ SIFTER ★

A sifter is good to have although not essential. It's often used for sifting confectioners' sugar over the cookies, and if you have a tea strainer that will do the job just as well.

★ PASTRY BRUSH ★

A brush is very handy for brushing away surplus flour, greasing pans, and brushing on egg or glazes. Buy a good quality brush that has firmly fixed bristles.

★ ROLLING PIN ★

Cookie dough is often rolled out to quite a large size so it is preferable to have a rolling pin that is straight and without handles. Other than that choose one that is comfortable for you.

★ CUTTERS ★

Some recipes require cutters. There are many cutters available in myriad shapes and sizes. For best results the cutter should be sharp and have a good clear outline. This generally means that they should be made of metal rather than plastic, but some plastic versions do have a sharp enough edge. To use a cutter, place gently on the dough and then using the palm of your hand press firmly and evenly down on the cutter. Lift the cutter off without twisting it. Some doughs may be slightly sticky or moist so it is a good idea to dip the edge of the cutter in some flour every now and then.

★ KNIVES ★

A large sharp knife is good for cutting cleanly through rolled out or refrigerated dough. Even more useful are a couple of round-bladed spatulas, one large, one small. They are invaluable for spreading and smoothing mixtures, transferring cut out cookies to baking sheets and removing them once cooked. They can also be used for spreading frosting or chocolate onto baked cookies.

★ PARCHMENT PAPER ★

A roll of parchment paper is good to have as it can be used to line baking sheets so cookies don't stick. It's also useful to sandwich soft or sticky dough when rolling out.

★ COOLING RACKS ★

These can be cheap and cheerful, it doesn't really matter. You can even use the grid from the broiler pan, but a cooling rack is necessary if you want crisp cookies as they will go soft if left on the baking sheet.

★ PASTRY BAGS & TIPS ★

Again, these are not essential as only a few recipes in the book require them but if you do a lot of baking they are useful to have. You can buy disposable pastry bags and plastic tips from most specialty kitchen stores.

★ AIRTIGHT STORAGE CONTAINERS ★

Homemade cookies can quickly lose their crispness in humid conditions so a few storage containers are vital.

INGREDIENTS

The finest ingredients make the finest cookies. Don't consider using up your shriveled dried fruit and musty old spices in a batch of cookies. Choose your ingredients carefully and you will have cookies to die for.

BUTTER

Most of the recipes are best made with unsalted butter. Out of all the ingredients (other then chocolate) butter has the most effect on the flavor and texture of cookies so use the best that you can afford. Avoid using tub margarines, butter substitutes, and spreads as these often contain a high percentage of water and will upset the balance of the recipe.

EGGS

Most of the recipes in this book use medium eggs unless stated otherwise. Farm fresh, organic, or free range eggs taste better and give a better result than battery eggs. Always use eggs at room temperature.

FLOUR

Flour does vary so always use a good premium brand and make sure it hasn't been hanging around too long. These days it is rare to find lumpy flour so sifting isn't always necessary but it does add more air, so making it easier to mix in. Don't sift whole-wheat flour as you will be taking out all the goodness.

BAKING POWDER & BAKING SODA

Some cookie recipes need extra help to rise and so need baking powder or baking soda or sometimes both. Make sure they are fresh as they go stale quite quickly once opened. If you have some that has been hanging around for a while it is best to throw it out and treat yourself to a new pack to avoid disappointing results.

SUGAR

Generally speaking unrefined pure cane sugars have a deeper flavor and are preferable to use but this is not as important as the type of sugar specified in the recipe. The sugar is usually chosen for a particular

reason. For example, superfine sugar has very small crystals which dissolve quickly and easily so it is ideal to use when creaming with fat. You can substitute the sugars in recipes but the results may not be as good.

CHOCOLATE

For the very best flavor always use bittersweet chocolate with at least 70% cocoa solids. Unless stated in the recipe never use chocolate chips to replace chocolate which is to be melted or blended into the batter as they are formulated to keep their shape when cooked and are sweeter and less smooth in texture. Some recipes call for milk or white chocolate so always look for the cooking variety and not confectionery bars.

LEMON & ORANGE ZEST

Always use unwaxed fruit, which has been washed before use.

SPICES & EXTRACTS

All spices should be as fresh as possible. Only buy in small quantities and if they don't smell wonderfully fresh when opened then buy some more. Always use a quality, pure extract, it really makes a difference.

FRUIT & NUTS

Dried fruit should be moist and plump. Fruits such as dates are often better bought whole rather than pre-chopped. Nuts should be as fresh as possible as the oils they contain can turn rancid. Store opened packages in the freezer if you are not going to use them regularly. When chopping or grinding nuts in a food processor always use a perfectly dry bowl and use the pulse button, scraping them down occasionally. Using this method there is no danger of the nuts turning into a paste.

MAKING COOKIES
with kids

Some of the first things young children learn to cook are little sweets, cakes, and cookies.

★ REASONS WHY ★

The recipes are simple and don't involve lots of hot pans and sharp knives which are too dangerous for very young children. Not only is baking fun, it can also be a useful lesson in many subjects. Measuring, weighing, and counting cookies is math; washing hands, keeping things clean and tidy is hygiene; seeing what happens when air is beaten into egg whites is science; and decorating with candies and frosting is creative art! So an afternoon spent baking is not frivolous but huge fun and very educational.

Fussy eaters can often be encouraged to be more adventurous if they are allowed to help with cooking. A savory cookie could be made for the child's lunch box—most children love eating the food they have made themselves.

Always allow plenty of time, especially when cooking with very young children, and remember they often lose interest but then come back a few minutes later. It is worth being patient at this stage as a love of cooking and food instilled at a young age is very valuable.

★ SAFETY TIPS ★

Remember a kitchen can sometimes be dangerous for children so there are a few things worth considering.

★ Young children run everywhere so make sure they wear shoes with non-slip soles—trainers are ideal.

★ An apron or even a clean dishtowel will protect their clothes from the food.

★ Make sure they wash their hands and tie back long hair. Keep a clean wet cloth handy for sticky fingers.

★ If they have to stand on a chair or stool to help, make sure it is secure—better if possible to let them mix and stir on a small table suitable to their height.

★ Place a wet cloth under mixing bowls and cutting boards as this will stop them from slipping.

★ Don't leave children alone with knives or electrical equipment.

★ A lot of the cookies in this book can be made much smaller—young children prefer tiny food. Just adjust the cooking time slightly.

★ Small children will find it easier to make drop cookies or those that they can roll into balls. Let older kids be creative with biscuits that are cut out and decorated.

★ The microwave is safer than the stove top for young children to use when doing such things as melting chocolate.

★ Gather all the ingredients together before you start as children are eager to get going but can lose interest if they are waiting around.

★ Encourage a little judicious tasting (avoiding raw egg) to experience new flavors and textures—you don't have to wait until the cookies are cooked. Remember licking out the bowl as a child?

TROUBLESHOOTING

Use these essential questions and answers to dig yourself out of any cookie baking problems you come across.

Q – *The recipe calls for softened butter, what is this?*

A – If you are using an electric mixer the butter should be left at room temperature until it gives slightly when pressed. If you are using a wooden spoon the butter should be the consistency of thick mayonnaise. Butter can be softened in the microwave at 30% power.

Q – *The first tray of cookies I bake are always OK but the cookies on subsequent trays are often deformed.*

A – Always cool cookie sheets before putting on a new batch of raw cookies. Warm sheets will start the dough melting slowly and this will cause the cookies to spread and become deformed.

Q – *I always find it difficult to measure very sticky ingredients such as corn syrup.*

A – To measure corn syrup and molasses accurately open the can or jar and rest the lid on top. Place the can or jar in a bowl and fill with boiling water to half way up the side of the can. Leave for a few minutes and then you will find the syrup is runny and easy to measure accurately.

Q – *I often find my dough to be very sticky and soft, so I add extra flour when rolling out, but then my biscuits turn out tough.*

A – Always refrigerate a dough rather than be tempted to add any extra flour. More flour equals a drier mixture, which will result in a tougher biscuit. Alternatively, roll out the dough between sheets of parchment paper.

Q – *My cookies always seem to bake unevenly.*

A – Always rotate the baking sheets half way through the baking time. If you are baking more than one sheet of cookies at a time then reverse them top to bottom and front to back. Also make sure all the cookies are the same size. If you are unsure of your oven you can fine tune the baking of cookies by test baking 3 or 4 cookies first.

Q – *How can I make sure my drop cookies are all even-sized?*

A – A good trick is to use a small round ice-cream scoop or lightly oiled measuring tablespoon.

Q – *I like to make cookies and usually make the drop variety—occasionally I would like to try other types but I don't have any cookie cutters.*

A – To cut cookie dough rounds without a cutter use a sturdy inverted wine glass. Or form small amounts of the dough into balls and flatten.

Q – *My cookies are often tough and dry, why is this?*

A – There could be a few reasons for this. Make sure your measuring is accurate. Do not over mix the dough once the flour has been added as this will cause the gluten to develop and create a tough cookie. The same applies to kneading and rolling out—keep it to a minimum and do not add extra flour. If the dough is sticky, chill it for a while and roll out between sheets of parchment paper. It could also be that you are leaving the cookies in the oven too long. Even a minute or two extra can make them dry and tough, so remove them just before you think they are done as they will continue to cook for a short time.

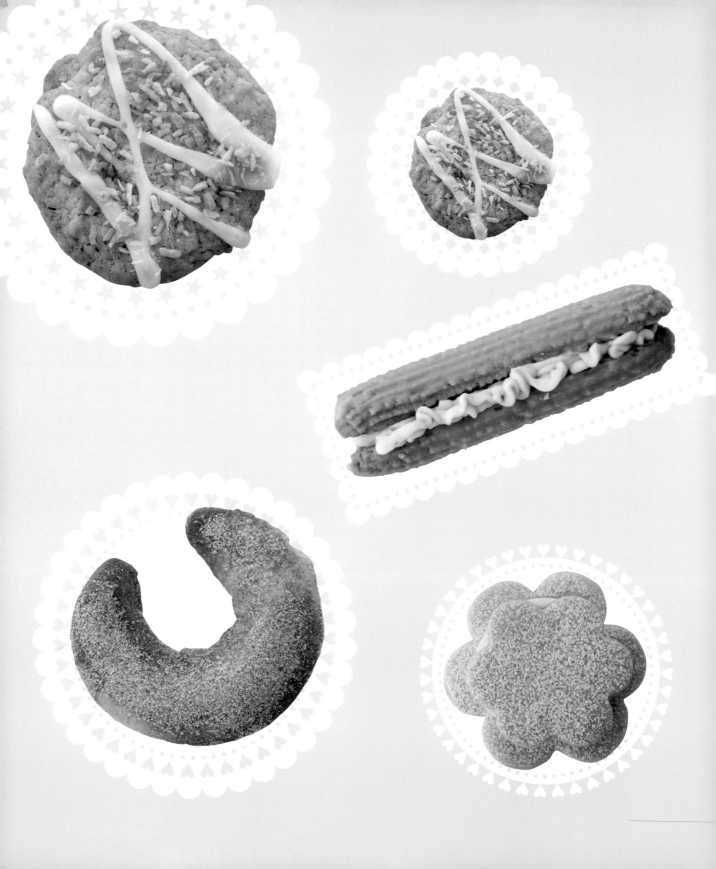

AFTERNOON
TEA

COCONUT Cookies

Rich cookies, with a strong coconut taste. Decorate them by dipping in chocolate or drizzling a little chocolate over the top.

MAKES: 24
BAKING TIME: 10–12 MINUTES

INGREDIENTS
¹/₂ cup/1 stick butter
Generous ³/₄ cup sugar
¹/₄ cup coconut milk
²/₃ cup flaked coconut
Generous 1¹/₂ cups all-purpose flour
2 teaspoons baking powder

FROSTING
Scant ¹/₄ cup confectioners' sugar
2 tablespoons coconut milk
Generous ¹/₂ cup flaked coconut

1. Preheat the oven to 350°F. Lightly grease two baking sheets.

2. Cream the butter and sugar together until pale and fluffy. Beat in the coconut milk and flaked coconut.

3. Sift the flour and baking powder and work into the coconut mixture. Drop tablespoons of the dough well apart on the baking sheets. Bake until golden, 10–12 minutes. Let cool on the baking sheets for 2–3 minutes, then transfer to a wire rack to cool completely.

4. To make the frosting, sift the confectioners' sugar into a bowl and stir in the coconut milk until smooth. Spread over the cookies, then sprinkle the coconut over the top. Let dry until the frosting sets, 1–2 hours. Store in an airtight container for up to five days.

BANANA & WALNUT Cookies

You could try using other types of nuts, but walnuts work particularly well with the smooth banana taste of these wholesome cookies.

MAKES: 20
BAKING TIME: 15 MINUTES

INGREDIENTS

Generous 1½ cups all-purpose flour
1 teaspoon baking powder
½ cup/1 stick butter, cut into cubes
⅞ cup light brown sugar
Scant 1 cup walnuts, coarsely chopped
2 small or 1 large banana, peeled
1 egg
¼ cup milk

1. Preheat the oven to 350°F. Lightly grease two baking sheets.

2. Sift the flour and baking powder into a bowl. Add the butter and blend with your fingertips until the mixture resembles fine bread crumbs. Stir in the sugar and walnuts.

3. Mash the banana with a fork and beat in the egg. Stir in the milk. Add to the bowl and mix until well combined.

4. Drop spoonfuls of the dough onto the baking sheets, spacing well apart. Bake until golden, about 15 minutes. Transfer to a wire rack to cool completely. Store in a cool place for up to three days. Suitable for freezing for up to two months.

COOKIE TIP
To make cookie sandwiches, melt some chocolate chips. Using a spatula, spread the chocolate over two cookies and then press them together.

CITRUS CREAM
Clouds

More like little cakes, these cookies would be good for special occasions such as a birthday tea.

MAKES: 18
BAKING TIME: 5–8 MINUTES

INGREDIENTS
³/₄ cup/1¹/₂ sticks butter
1 teaspoon finely grated lime zest
¹/₂ cup confectioners' sugar
2 cups all-purpose flour
¹/₃ cup cornstarch
Confectioners' sugar for dusting

FILLING
¹/₂ cup/1 stick unsalted butter at room temperature
1 teaspoon vanilla extract
1 teaspoon finely grated orange zest
1 teaspoon finely grated lemon zest
1 cup confectioners' sugar, sifted

1. Beat together the butter, lime zest, and confectioners' sugar until smooth and creamy. Stir in the flour and cornstarch and knead until smooth. Wrap in plastic wrap and chill for 30 minutes until firm.

2. Roll out half the dough between sheets of parchment paper. Using a flower-shaped cutter or a cutter of your choice cut out eighteen 1¹/₂-inch shapes.

3. Add any scraps of dough to the remaining pastry and roll out as before and cut out eighteen 2¹/₂-inch shapes.

4. Preheat the oven to 350°F. Place the shapes 1 inch apart on baking sheets lined with parchment paper. Bake in the oven for about 5–6 minutes for small shapes and 7–8 for large shapes, until lightly browned. Place on wire racks to cool.

5. Put all the filling ingredients into a bowl and beat together until smooth and creamy.

6. Either pipe or spread the filling on each of the larger cookies. Top each one with a smaller cookie. Dust with confectioners' sugar to serve.

GINGER Crisps

These crisp ginger cookies look very impressive. You will need to work quickly, but once you get the hang of them, they are quite easy to make.

MAKES: 20
BAKING TIME: 5–6 MINUTES

INGREDIENTS
¼ cup/½ stick butter
Scant ½ cup all-purpose flour
1½ teaspoons ground ginger
½ teaspoon ground cinnamon
¼ teaspoon ground cloves
½ cup packed brown sugar
2 egg whites

1. Preheat the oven to 375°F. Lightly grease two baking sheets.

2. Melt the butter gently in a pan, then let it cool but not solidify.

3. Sift the flour and spices together, then sift again to ensure that they are well mixed and lightly aerated. Sift the brown sugar to remove any lumps.

4. Beat the egg whites until they stand in soft peaks. Gradually beat in the sugar. Carefully fold in the flour mixture. Drizzle in the butter and fold until just combined.

5. Place 2–3 heaping teaspoons of the dough onto a baking sheet and spread each one to form a 3-inch circle. Bake until just set and beginning to brown around the edges, 5–6 minutes. While one batch of cookies is cooking, spread the next one on the second baking sheet. Oil a rolling pin.

6. When baked, let the cookies stand for a few seconds. Then, working quickly before they set, carefully remove from the baking sheet with a slim spatula and place over the oiled rolling pin; they will cool in a curve. Remove from the rolling pin. Repeat until all the dough is baked. Store in an airtight container for two to three days.

LEMON MACADAMIA NUT Cookies —OK

These cookies have a lovely lemon tang.
They are fabulous served with creamy desserts.

MAKES: 24
BAKING TIME: 10–12 MINUTES

INGREDIENTS

½ cup/1 stick butter, softened
½ cup sugar
2 egg yolks
Grated zest of ½ lemon
¼ cup lemon juice
Generous 1½ cups all-purpose flour
6 tablespoons cornstarch
Scant 1 cup macadamia nuts, lightly
    chopped

1. Preheat the oven to 375°F. Lightly grease two baking sheets.

2. Cream the butter and sugar together until light and fluffy. Beat in the egg yolks, lemon zest, and juice.

3. Sift the flour and cornstarch and beat into the mixture. Add the nuts and stir until well mixed.

4. Drop heaping tablespoons of the dough onto the baking sheets and flatten slightly with the back of a spoon.

5. Bake until golden, 10–12 minutes. Let cool on the baking sheets for a few minutes before transferring to a wire rack to cool completely.

sift Powdered sugar ontop when cooled

COOKIE TIP
If a recipe calls for both lemon zest and juice, pour the lemon juice over the zest to keep it moist.

MALTED DROP Cookies

These have a great malty flavor and a chewy texture.
Perfect served with a cup of steaming hot cocoa.

MAKES: 18
BAKING TIME: 10–12 MINUTES

INGREDIENTS

½ cup/1 stick butter, softened
Scant ½ cup sugar
1 egg, lightly beaten
1 teaspoon vanilla extract
5 tablespoons chocolate malt powder
Scant ¾ cup all-purpose flour
½ cup rolled oats

COOKIE TIP
To prevent parchment paper slipping off baking sheets, sprinkle the baking sheet with a few drops of water beforehand.

1. Preheat the oven to 375°F. Line two baking sheets with nonstick parchment paper.

2. Cream the butter and sugar together until light and fluffy. Beat in the egg and vanilla. Sift the chocolate malt powder and flour together and beat into the creamed mixture along with the oats until all the ingredients are well combined.

3. Drop heaping teaspoons of the dough onto the baking sheets, spacing well apart. Bake in the center of the oven until just golden, 10–12 minutes. The lower baking sheet may need slightly longer. Let the cookies cool on the baking sheets for a few minutes, then transfer to a wire rack to cool completely.

SPICY BUTTERMILK
Cookies

The pumpkin pie spice and tangy buttermilk
in these cookies lends a sweet and gentle kick.

MAKES: 20
BAKING TIME: 10–15 MINUTES

INGREDIENTS

6 tablespoons/³⁄₄ stick butter,
   softened
²⁄₃ cup sugar
²⁄₃ cup buttermilk
Generous 1¹⁄₂ cups all-purpose flour
¹⁄₂ teaspoon baking soda
2 teaspoons pumpkin pie spice

1. Preheat the oven to 400°F. Lightly grease two baking sheets.

2. Cream the butter and sugar together in a bowl until light and fluffy. Beat in the buttermilk. Sift the flour, baking soda, and spice together and beat into the creamed mixture.

3. Drop rounded tablespoons of the dough onto the baking sheets, spacing well apart as the cookies will almost double in size.

4. Bake until golden, 10–15 minutes. Let cool on the baking sheets for a few minutes before transferring to a wire rack to cool completely.

COOKIE TIP
*If you prefer not
to use buttermilk,
yogurt is a very good
substitute.*

BASIC SPRITZ
Cookies

Spritz cookies are a firm family favorite and perfect for popping in the mouth at any time. The name derives from the German verb spritzen, meaning "squirt" or to "spray."

MAKES: 24–30
BAKING TIME: 8–10 MINUTES

INGREDIENTS
½ cup/1 stick butter, softened
Scant 1 cup confectioners' sugar
1 egg
½ teaspoon vanilla extract
Generous 1⅔ cups all-purpose flour
Colored sugar crystals for decoration

1. Preheat the oven to 400°F. Lightly grease two baking sheets.

2. Cream the butter and sugar together until light and fluffy. Beat in the egg and vanilla. Fold in the flour.

3. If using a cookie press, chill the dough for about 30 minutes until firm but not hard. Press the cookies onto baking sheets. If you do not have a cookie press you can pipe the cookies, but do not chill the dough first.

4. Decorate with colored sugar crystals and bake until lightly golden, about 8–10 minutes. Let cool on the baking sheets for a few minutes before transferring to a wire rack to cool completely.

COOKIE TIP
Cool cookies on wire racks without touching each other to keep them from sticking together.

CHOCOLATE MINT Creams

A wonderful combination of crisp mint and warm sweet chocolate. If you prefer you could substitute the peppermint extract for orange extract to make Chocolate Orange Creams.

1. Cream the butter and sugar together until light and fluffy. Sift together the flour and cocoa powder and beat in until smooth. Form into a 2-inch thick log and let chill for 1 hour.

2. Preheat the oven to 375°F. Lightly grease two baking sheets. Cut the log into slices ¼ inch thick and arrange well apart on baking sheets. Bake until just firm, about 8 minutes.

3. Let the cookies cool on the baking sheets for a few minutes before transferring to a wire rack to cool completely.

4. To make the filling, place the cream in a mixing bowl and beat in the confectioners' sugar. Add peppermint extract to taste.

5. Sandwich pairs of cookies together with the filling. Store in a cool place for up to three days.

MAKES: 18
BAKING TIME: 8 MINUTES

INGREDIENTS
¾ cup/1½ sticks butter, softened
¼ cup sugar
Scant 1⅓ cups all-purpose flour
2 tablespoons unsweetened cocoa
    powder

FILLING
2 tablespoons milk or light cream
Scant 1 cup confectioners' sugar
½–1 teaspoon peppermint extract

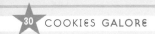

CHOCOLATE & PISTACHIO Fingers

Softer than normal shortbread these cookies are good served with tea or coffee.

MAKES: **12**
BAKING TIME: **15 MINUTES**

INGREDIENTS

Scant 1 cup unsalted butter
½ cup golden superfine sugar
2 ¼ cups all-purpose flour
½ cup unsweetened cocoa powder
¼ cup shelled pistachio nuts, coarsely
 chopped
Unsweetened cocoa powder for
 dusting

1. Preheat the oven to 350°F. Line a shallow square 7-inch pan with parchment paper.

2. Cream the butter and sugar together until light and fluffy. Sift together the flour and cocoa powder. Add to the butter mixture and work in using your hands until the mixture is smooth. Add the pistachios and knead until soft and pliable.

3. Press the mixture into the pan and smooth the top using the back of a tablespoon. Prick with a fork and mark into bars.

4. Bake in the oven for about 15 minutes. Do not allow to become too brown or the cookies will taste bitter.

5. Allow to cool slightly then cut through the marked sections and remove from the pan. Cool on a wire rack and dust sparingly with cocoa powder.

HONEY & LEMON Cookies

To make these cookies more attractive, you could use star-shaped cutters to give a more sophisticated finish.

MAKES: 16
BAKING TIME: 10–12 MINUTES

INGREDIENTS
Generous 1²/₃ cups all-purpose flour
1 teaspoon baking soda
Scant ¹/₄ cup sugar
Grated zest and juice of 1 lemon
¹/₂ cup/1 stick butter
5 tablespoons honey
FILLING
4 tablespoons butter, softened
²/₃ cup confectioners' sugar
2 tablespoons honey
2 teaspoons lemon juice

1. Sift the flour and baking soda into a bowl. Stir in the sugar and lemon zest. Blend in the butter until the mixture resembles fine bread crumbs.

2. Heat the honey and lemon juice in a small pan until very runny but not too hot. Pour into the flour mixture and mix to form a soft dough. Chill for 30 minutes or until firm enough to handle. Preheat the oven to 375°F. Lightly grease a baking sheet.

3. Roll the dough into small balls and arrange well spaced on the baking sheet. Flatten slightly with a knife. Bake until golden brown, 10–12 minutes.

4. Let cool on the baking sheet for a few minutes before transferring to a wire rack to cool completely.

5. To make the filling, cream the butter and confectioners' sugar together until light and fluffy. Beat in the honey and lemon juice. Sandwich the cookies together in pairs with the filling.

LADY GREY TEA Cookies

The unusual ingredient in these cookies is Lady Grey tea—similar to Earl Grey but with the addition of Seville orange and lemon peel.

MAKES: 18–20
BAKING TIME: 10–15 MINUTES

INGREDIENTS
1/3 cup/2/3 stick unsalted butter, at
   room temperature
1/4 cup light brown sugar
1 tablespoon Lady Grey tea leaves
1 egg white
1 1/3 cups all-purpose flour
TOPPING
Demerara sugar

1. Preheat the oven to 375°F. Line baking sheets with parchment paper.

2. Put the butter and sugar into a bowl and beat together until creamy. Stir in the tea leaves.

3. Beat in the egg white. Fold in the flour to make a soft but not sticky dough. On a lightly floured surface roll into a cylinder. Flatten slightly to make a cross section that looks like a finger biscuit with rounded ends. Wrap carefully in plastic wrap and chill until firm enough to slice.

4. Cut into thin slices and place on the prepared baking sheets. Sprinkle each biscuit with Demerara sugar. Bake in the oven for 10–15 minutes until lightly browned.

COOKIE TIP
Store delicate cookies between sheets of waxed paper for safe keeping.

NUTTY JELLY
Slices

Sticky and crunchy, these bite-size slices are enjoyable to make and great for teatime snacking.

1. Lightly grease a baking sheet. Cream the butter and sugar together until light and fluffy. Beat in the egg yolk and almond extract. Work in the flour and ground almonds to form a firm dough. Add a little extra flour if the mixture is too soft.

2. Divide the dough in half and roll each into a log about 10 inches long. Place on the prepared sheet.

3. Lightly beat the egg white with a fork and brush over each log. Lightly crush the almonds and press onto the logs. Flatten each log slightly. Use the handle of a wooden spoon to press a channel down the center of each log. Fill the hollows with jelly. Let chill for 30 minutes.

4. Preheat the oven to 350°F.

5. Bake the logs until pale golden brown, 10–12 minutes. Leave on the baking sheet until the jam has set but the dough is still warm. Cut diagonally into slices and transfer to a wire rack to cool completely.

MAKES: 20
BAKING TIME: 10–12 MINUTES

INGREDIENTS
$\frac{1}{4}$ cup/$\frac{1}{2}$ stick butter
Scant $\frac{1}{4}$ cup sugar
1 egg, separated
1 teaspoon almond extract
Scant $\frac{2}{3}$ cup all-purpose flour
Scant $\frac{1}{4}$ cup ground almonds
Scant $\frac{1}{4}$ cup sliced almonds
Jelly of your choice

COFFEE & CINNAMON Cookies

The cinnamon flavor and attractive crescent shape of these little cookies makes them perfect for serving at Christmas time.

MAKES: 40
BAKING TIME: 12 MINUTES

INGREDIENTS
1 tablespoon instant coffee granules
1 tablespoon boiling water
1 cup/2 sticks butter
Scant ¾ cup sugar
1 tablespoon Kahlúa or other coffee-
    flavored liqueur
Scant 3 cups all-purpose flour
2 teaspoons ground cinnamon
¼ cup confectioners' sugar

1. Preheat the oven to 350°F. Lightly grease two baking sheets. Dissolve the coffee in 1 tablespoon boiling water.

2. Cream the butter and sugar together until pale and fluffy. Beat in the coffee and liqueur. Sift the flour and 1 teaspoon of the cinnamon together, then beat into the dough.

3. Take small amounts of the dough, each about the size of a walnut, and roll into balls. Shape each ball into a log, then curve it into a crescent. Space well apart on the baking sheets. Bake until golden, about 12 minutes. Let cool on the baking sheets for 2–3 minutes, then transfer to a wire rack to cool completely.

4. Sift the confectioners' sugar and remaining cinnamon together a few times to ensure that the sugar and spice are well mixed. Dust the cookies with the spiced sugar. Store in an airtight container for up to five days.

BUTTERSCOTCH

Fingers

A variation on the Viennese finger these cookies have a delicious butterscotch flavor and a delightful crisp coating.

MAKES: 9
BAKING TIME: 8–10 MINUTES

INGREDIENTS
1 cup/2 sticks unsalted butter
½ cup dark brown sugar, firmly packed
1 egg white
1¾ cups all-purpose flour
BUTTERSCOTCH CREAM
2 tablespoons butter
1 tablespoon cream
1 cup golden confectioners' sugar, sifted
GLAZE
⅞ cup golden confectioners' sugar

1. Preheat the oven to 350°F. Beat the butter and sugar together until light and fluffy. Beat in the egg white. Stir in the flour and mix well.

2. Spoon the mixture into a pastry bag fitted with a ½-inch star tip and pipe eighteen 3½-inch long fingers on lightly greased baking sheets.

3. Bake for about 8–10 minutes or until lightly browned. Cool on a wire rack.

4. To make the glaze, put the confectioners' sugar into a small bowl and add enough water to mix to a pouring consistency. Using a pastry brush, spread the glaze over each biscuit and allow to dry.

5. To make the filling, put the ingredients into a bowl and beat together until smooth. Sandwich the biscuits together with a little of the butterscotch cream.

COOKIE TIP
Make sure you allow the glaze to dry and the filling to set before storing in an airtight container.

ALMOND & VANILLA
FUDGE Crumbles

Crumbly almond cookies with a crunchy topping
have the surprise addition of tiny pieces of fudge.

MAKES: 24
BAKING TIME: 10–12 MINUTES

INGREDIENTS
1½ cups self-rising flour
Pinch of salt
½ cup/1 stick sweet butter
½ cup light brown sugar
1 egg
1 teaspoon almond extract
⅓ cup ground almonds
2 ounces vanilla cream fudge, finely
   diced
TOPPING
2 tablespoons flaked almonds,
   crumbled
2 tablespoons Demerara sugar

1. Sift the flour and salt into a bowl. Blend in the butter. Add all the remaining ingredients (except those for the topping) and mix to a fairly firm dough. Wrap in plastic wrap. Chill for 15 minutes.

2. Preheat the oven to 375°F. Divide the dough into 24 pieces and place, slightly apart on baking sheets lined with parchment paper.

3. To make the topping: mix together the flaked almonds and Demerara sugar and sprinkle a little on top of each cookie, pressing down lightly using the back of a spoon.

4. Bake in the oven for about 10–12 minutes until turning golden at the edges.

5. Remove from the oven and allow to cool for 5 minutes before removing to a wire rack.

GYPSY Creams

A crisp chocolate oat cookie encases a creamy chocolate filling in these hearty, classic, and wholesome sandwich cookies.

MAKES: 10
BAKING TIME: 20 MINUTES

INGREDIENTS
¼ cup/½ stick butter, softened
¼ cup white vegetable shortening
Scant ¼ cup sugar
Scant ⅔ cup all-purpose flour
½ cup rolled oats
1 tablespoon unsweetened cocoa
   powder

FILLING
¼ cup/½ stick butter, softened
⅔ cup confectioners' sugar
2 tablespoons unsweetened cocoa
   powder

1. Preheat the oven to 350°F. Lightly grease a baking sheet.

2. Cream the butter, shortening, and sugar together until light and fluffy. Beat in the remaining ingredients.

3. Roll the dough into small balls and place on the baking sheet. Flatten with a fork dipped in hot water. Bake until golden, about 20 minutes. Let cool on the baking sheet.

4. To make the filling, cream the butter until fluffy, then gradually beat in the confectioners' sugar and cocoa powder. Sandwich the cookies together in pairs with the filling.

TROPICAL FRUIT
Cookies

Soft cookies packed with tropical fruit
and topped with coconut frosting.

MAKES: 16–18
BAKING TIME: 12 MINUTES

INGREDIENTS
½ cup/1 stick butter
⅓ cup superfine sugar
1 egg
1⅓ cups self-rising flour
⅓ cup ground almonds
9-ounce pack ready-to-eat tropical
  fruit mix, chopped
FROSTING
1 cup confectioners' sugar
2–3 tablespoons coconut cream

1. Preheat the oven to 350°F.
Put the butter and sugar into a bowl
and beat together until creamy.
Beat in the egg.

2. Stir in the flour, ground almonds
and fruit. Place spoonfuls of the
mixture 2 inches apart on a nonstick
baking sheet.

3. Bake in the oven for about 12 minutes or
until lightly browned. Cool on a wire rack.

4. To make the frosting: sift the confectioners' sugar into a bowl. Add the
coconut cream and mix until thick but not too runny. Spoon over the
cookies and leave to set.

COOKIE TIP
*Only store one kind
of cookie in a container.
If you mix crisp and soft
cookies they will all go
soft and end up tasting
the same.*

FRUITY OAT
Bites

These are perfect as a healthy afternoon snack as the dried fruit will give long-lasting energy.

MAKES: 10
BAKING TIME: 20–25 MINUTES

INGREDIENTS
¾ cup/1¼ sticks butter
⅓ cup light brown sugar
⅓ cup honey
6 ounces granola
¼ cup rolled oats
½ cup chopped dried apricots
½ cup chopped dried apple
½ cup chopped dried mango

1. Preheat the oven to 375°F. Lightly grease an 8 x 8-inch square pan and line the bottom with nonstick parchment paper.

2. Melt the butter, sugar, and honey together in a saucepan, stirring until well combined. Remove from the heat and stir in the granola, oats, apricots, apple, and mango.

3. Press the mixture into the prepared cake pan. Bake for 20–25 minutes.

4. Allow to cool for a few minutes in the pan, then cut into bars. Allow to cool completely in the pan before serving. Store in an airtight container for up to two weeks.

LUNCHBOX

CHOC CHIP & MIXED NUT Cookies

A classic recipe for all the family that produces a chewy, melt-in-the-mouth cookie, just like Grandma used to make.

MAKES: 10–12
BAKING TIME: 15–18 MINUTES

INGREDIENTS
1 cup/2 sticks butter, softened
Generous ³/₄ cup sugar
³/₄ cup brown sugar, lightly packed
2 eggs
1 teaspoon vanilla extract
Generous 1³/₄ cups all-purpose flour
1 teaspoon baking soda
1 cup semisweet or milk chocolate chips
Scant ³/₄ cup mixed nuts (walnuts, pecans, almonds, hazelnuts etc.), chopped

1. Preheat the oven to 325°F. Lightly grease two baking sheets.

2. Cream the butter and sugars together until light and fluffy. Beat in the eggs and vanilla. Sift the flour with the baking soda and beat into the mixture. Add the chocolate chips and nuts and stir until well combined.

3. Drop large rounded tablespoons of the dough onto the baking sheets, five or six per sheet, well spaced as the cookies will spread.

4. Bake until golden, 15–18 minutes. Let cool on the baking sheets for a few minutes before transferring to a wire rack to cool completely.

COOKIE TIP
Only grease the baking sheets when the recipe instructs you to. Otherwise the cookies may spread too much and become flat.

ORANGE & PEANUT BUTTER Cookies

The combination of zesty orange and rich peanut butter
in this recipe makes for a fresh yet wholesome, tasty cookie.

MAKES: **24**
BAKING TIME: **18–20 MINUTES**

INGREDIENTS
$\frac{1}{2}$ cup/1 stick butter, softened
Scant $\frac{1}{2}$ cup sugar
1 egg, lightly beaten
$\frac{1}{4}$ cup peanut butter
Grated zest of 1 small orange
$\frac{1}{4}$ cup orange juice
2 cups all-purpose flour
1 teaspoon baking powder

1. Preheat the oven to 350°F. Lightly grease two baking sheets.

2. Cream the butter and sugar together until light and fluffy. Beat in the egg, peanut butter, orange zest, and juice. Sift the flour and baking powder together and beat into the mixture.

3. Drop rounded tablespoons of the dough, spaced well apart onto the baking sheets. Flatten slightly with the back of a spoon.

4. Bake until golden, 18–20 minutes. Let cool on the baking sheets for a few minutes before transferring to a wire rack to cool completely.

COOKIE TIP
For even baking, always bake cookies on the middle rack of your oven.

TRADITIONAL CHOC CHIP Cookies

Enjoy the contrast of white and semisweet chocolate chips in this delicious twist on everyone's favorite cookie.

MAKES: 14
BAKING TIME: 12–15 MINUTES

INGREDIENTS

2 ounces semisweet chocolate chips
2 ounces white chocolate chips
1¼ sticks butter
²⁄₃ cup sugar
1 egg
½ teaspoon vanilla extract
1⅓ cups all-purpose flour
1 teaspoon baking powder

1. Preheat the oven to 350°F. Lightly grease two baking sheets.

2. Cream the butter and sugar together until pale and fluffy. Beat in the egg and the vanilla. Sift the flour and baking powder together and beat into the mixture. Add the chocolate chips and stir until well combined.

3. Drop 5–6 rounded tablespoons of the dough onto each baking sheet, spacing well apart, as the cookies will almost double in size.

4. Bake until golden, 12–15 minutes. Let cool on the baking sheet for 2–3 minutes, then transfer to a wire rack to cool completely. Store in an airtight container for up to five days.

COOKIE TIP
Never drop cookies on to a hot baking sheet. Use two baking sheets if instructed to, or cool the sheet in between batches.

OATMEAL CHOC CHIP Cookies

For an old-fashioned, coarser texture, be sure to use rolled oats. However, if you prefer a smoother cookie, use quick-cooking oats.

MAKES: 10–12
BAKING TIME: 8–10 MINUTES

INGREDIENTS

Generous 1 cup all-purpose flour
1 teaspoon baking powder
¾ cup/1½ sticks unsalted butter, softened
½ cup dark brown sugar, firmly packed
Scant ½ cup sugar
1 large egg, at room temperature
2 teaspoons vanilla extract
2½ cups rolled oats
Scant ½ cup semisweet chocolate chips

1. Preheat the oven to 375°F. Lightly grease two baking sheets.

2. In a large bowl, stir together the flour and baking powder.

3. In a large mixing bowl and using a hand-held electric mixer, cream the butter and sugars together until light and fluffy. Add the egg and beat until combined. Stir in the vanilla. With the mixer on low speed or using a wooden spoon, gradually add the flour mixture until combined. Stir in the oats and the chocolate chips.

4. Drop rounded tablespoonfuls of the dough, well spaced apart onto the baking sheets. Leave space between each one for spreading. Flatten each cookie slightly with the back of the spoon. Bake until golden for 12–15 minutes.

5. Remove the cookies from the baking sheets to a wire rack and let cool.

GINGER & DATE SANDWICH Cookies

Ginger and date makes for a great combination, however, you might like to replace the filling with raisins or even dried apricots instead of dates.

MAKES: 14
BAKING TIME: 12–15 MINUTES

INGREDIENTS
½ cup/1 stick butter
Scant ½ cup sugar
1 tablespoon light corn syrup
Generous 1½ cups all-purpose flour
1 teaspoon ground ginger
½ teaspoon baking powder
FILLING:
Generous ½ cup pitted dates
¼ cup sugar
⅓ cup water

1. Preheat the oven to 375°F. Lightly grease two baking sheets.

2. Place the butter, sugar, and syrup in a pan and heat gently, stirring, until the butter melts. Remove from the heat. Sift the flour, ginger, and baking powder together and stir into the butter mixture to form a dough.

3. Roll the dough into small balls and arrange on the baking sheets. Flatten slightly with a knife. Bake until golden, 12–15 minutes. Let cool on a wire rack.

4. To make the filling, chop the dates. Place in a pan with the sugar and water. Heat gently, stirring, until the sugar dissolves. Bring to a boil, then reduce the heat and cook gently for about 15 minutes until the mixture reduces to a thick, spreadable paste. Remove from the heat and let cool.

5. Use the date mixture to sandwich the ginger cookies together in pairs. Store in an airtight container for up to four days.

CHERRY & CHOCOLATE NUT Slices

Although macadamia nuts taste wonderful alongside the cherries, hazelnuts would work equally well.

MAKES: 9

INGREDIENTS
7 ounces unsweetened chocolate
½ cup/1 stick butter
½ cup light corn syrup
12 ounces gingersnap cookies
1 cup candied cherries
Generous ¾ cup coarsely chopped, toasted macadamias

1. Coarsely chop the chocolate and butter and place in a large bowl with the corn syrup. Melt by microwaving on medium for 2 minutes or by setting the bowl over a pan of simmering water.

2. Place half the gingersnaps in a food processor and process to fine crumbs. Coarsely chop the remaining cookies and add both to the melted chocolate mixture. Halve the cherries and add with the nuts to the chocolate mixture. Combine thoroughly so that the cookies, cherries, and nuts are coated with chocolate.

3. Line an 8 x 8-inch removable bottomed square cake pan with nonstick parchment paper. Spoon in the chocolate mixture and let set in the refrigerator for 2 hours. Remove from the pan, peel off the paper, and cut into slices.

LEMON Thins

The tangy cream cheese of the filling contrasts beautifully with the zesty lemon of this cookie.

MAKES: 20
BAKING TIME: 8 MINUTES

INGREDIENTS
1¼ cups all-purpose flour
3½ tablespoons cornstarch
½ cup/1 stick butter
Scant ½ cup confectioners' sugar
Grated zest of ½ lemon
1 tablespoon lemon juice
FILLING
Scant ½ cup cream cheese
Scant ½ cup confectioners' sugar
¼ cup lemon curd

1. Preheat the oven to 400°F. Lightly grease two baking sheets. Sift the flour and cornstarch into a mixing bowl. Cut the butter into small pieces and blend into the flour until the mixture resembles fine bread crumbs.

2. Stir in the confectioners' sugar and lemon zest. Add the lemon juice, then bring the mixture together with your hands to form a soft dough. Chill for 20 minutes.

3. On a lightly floured counter, roll out the dough as thin as possible and cut into circles with a 2-inch cookie cutter. Arrange on the baking sheets and bake until crisp and golden, about 8 minutes. Let cool on the baking sheets for 2 3 minutes, then transfer to a wire rack to cool completely.

4. For the filling, beat together the cream cheese, confectioners' sugar, and lemon curd. Sandwich together pairs of cookies with the filling. Store in an airtight container in a cool place for up to three days.

COOKIE TIP
Baked and uncooked shaped cookies can be frozen for up to two months. Thaw baked cookies at room temperature and bake uncooked ones from frozen.

CARAMELITAS

The unbeatable combination of chocolate and caramel makes these bars a firm favorite.

MAKES: 20
BAKING TIME: 20–25 MINUTES

INGREDIENTS

2 cups rolled oats

2 cups all-purpose flour

1 teaspoon baking soda

1 1/2 cups light brown sugar

1/2 teaspoon salt

1 cup/2 sticks unsalted butter, melted

10 ounces bittersweet chocolate, coarsely chopped

1 cup pecans, lightly toasted and coarsely chopped

1 cup caramel sauce (or Dulce de Leche)

1. Preheat the oven to 350°F. Base line a 12 x 12-inch shallow baking pan with parchment paper.

2. Put the oats, flour, baking soda, sugar, and salt into a bowl and mix together. Add the butter and mix well. Spread half of the mixture in the base of the prepared pan. Press out evenly using the back of a spoon.

3. Bake in the oven for 10 minutes. Remove and sprinkle the chocolate and nuts evenly over the surface. Drizzle the caramel sauce evenly over the top. Sprinkle the reserved oat mixture on top and press gently with the back of a spoon.

4. Bake in the oven for 20–25 minutes until golden brown.

5. Leave in the pan to cool completely and cut into bars to serve.

COOKIE TIP

You can always vary nuts in recipes to suit personal taste. Pecans could be substituted with walnuts and almonds with hazelnuts for example.

SNICKERDOODLES

A soft traditional cookie, with a funny name, originating from 19th-century New England.

MAKES: 36
BAKING TIME: 8–10 MINUTES

INGREDIENTS
¾ cup/1½ sticks butter, softened
1 cup sugar
1 egg
1 teaspoon vanilla extract
Scant 2 cups all-purpose flour
1 teaspoon cream of tartar
½ teaspoon baking soda

COATING
1 tablespoon sugar
1 teaspoon ground cinnamon

1. Preheat the oven to 400°F. Lightly grease two baking sheets.

2. Cream the butter and the sugar together until light and fluffy. Beat in the egg and vanilla. Sift the flour, cream of tartar, and baking soda together and blend into the butter mixture to form a soft dough.

3. Break off pieces of the dough about the size of a small walnut and roll into balls. Mix the 1 tablespoon sugar and cinnamon together and roll each ball in the cinnamon sugar. Arrange on the baking sheets, allowing room for the cookies to spread.

4. Bake until pale golden, about 8–10 minutes. Transfer to a wire rack to cool.

COOKIE TIP
You could also try making whole-wheat snickerdoodles by substituting 1 cup whole-wheat flour for 1 cup of the all-purpose flour.

SPICED Pretzels

With a lovely spicy flavor and unusual shape, these pretzels are sure to impress guests when offered as a savory snack at a drinks party or impromptu get-together.

1. Preheat the oven to 350°F. Lightly grease two baking sheets.

2. Sift the flour, baking powder, and salt into a mixing bowl and blend in the butter until the mixture resembles fine bread crumbs. Stir the curry paste into ¼ cup boiling water, then add to the flour mixture and mix to form a soft dough.

3. Knead on a lightly floured counter until smooth. Divide into 30 pieces and roll each piece into a strand about 8 inches long. Twist into a pretzel shape by making a circle, then twisting the ends around each other to form a curved letter "B." Press into position to secure and place on the baking sheets.

4. Brush the pretzels with beaten egg. Bake until golden, 18–20 minutes. Carefully transfer to a wire rack to cool.

5. Store in an airtight container for one to two weeks.

MAKES: 30
BAKING TIME: 18–20 MINUTES

INGREDIENTS
Scant 1⅓ cups all-purpose flour
½ teaspoon baking powder
Pinch of salt
6 tablespoons/¾ stick butter
1 tablespoon curry paste
¼ cup boiling water
Beaten egg, to glaze

SAVORY
Whirls

You can leave these plain or top with a selection of olives, anchovies, marinated bell peppers, nuts, or sun-dried tomatoes.

MAKES: 15
BAKING TIME: 12–15 MINUTES

INGREDIENTS
½ cup/1 stick butter, softened
1 clove garlic, crushed
2 tablespoons sour cream
Generous 1 cup all-purpose flour
½ teaspoon paprika
Salt and freshly ground black pepper

1. Preheat the oven to 375°F. Lightly grease two baking sheets.

2. Cream the butter until soft, then beat in the garlic, sour cream, flour, paprika, and seasoning. Mix to form a smooth paste.

3. Spoon into a pastry bag fitted with a large star tip and pipe rosettes onto the baking sheets.

4. Bake until golden, 12–15 minutes. Let cool on the baking sheets for a few minutes before transferring to a wire rack to cool completely.

COOKIE TIP
Always measure ingredients accurately. Use glass measuring cups for liquid ingredients as it is more accurate to see the level of liquid.

SAVORY PALMIER
Cookies

These cookies are so versatile—spread them with whatever filling you choose. A little cheese sprinkled over the olives works well.

1. Preheat the oven to 400°F. Roll out the pastry on a lightly floured counter to form a 10 x 12-inch rectangle. Trim the edges with a sharp knife.

2. Spread the pesto in a thin layer all over the pastry, taking care to go right to the edges. Sprinkle with the chopped olives. With the long side facing you, fold about 3 inches of the shorter sides of the pastry so that they reach about half way toward the center. Fold again so that they just meet in the center. Lightly dampen the pastry with a little water and fold again in half down the center.

3. Using a sharp knife, cut the roll into about 20 thin slices and arrange cut-side down, well spaced, on the baking sheets.

4. Bake for 10 minutes, then turn them over and bake until golden and crisp, 5–8 minutes. Transfer to a wire rack to cool.

MAKES: 20
BAKING TIME: 15–18 MINUTES

INGREDIENTS
9 ounces ready-made puff pastry, thawed if frozen
2 tablespoons pesto
Generous $\frac{1}{4}$ cup pitted black olives, finely chopped

COOKIE TIP
Palmiers are best served slightly warm, however, if this is not possible, room temperature is fine.

SESAME CHEESE Twists

These classic twists are a favorite at parties and look very professional—however, they are actually unbelievably easy to make!

MAKES: 14
BAKING TIME: 10–12 MINUTES

INGREDIENTS
4 ounces cheddar cheese
½ cup/1 stick butter, softened
Scant 1⅓ cups all-purpose flour
Beaten egg, to glaze
2 tablespoons sesame seeds

1. Preheat the oven to 400°F. Lightly grease two baking sheets. Finely grate the cheese, using the fine grater attachment of a food processor.

2. Remove the grating disc and insert the metal mixing blade. Place the butter in the food processor with the cheese and process until pale and creamy. Add the flour and process until the mixture comes together to form a ball of dough.

3. Roll out the dough on a lightly floured counter to about ⅛ inch thick. Cut into strips about 6 inches long and ¼ inch wide. Take two strips at a time and twist together, pinching the ends.

4. Arrange on the baking sheets. Brush with beaten egg and sprinkle with sesame seeds. Bake until pale golden, 10–12 minutes. Let cool for a few minutes on the baking sheets, then transfer to a wire rack to cool completely. Store in an airtight container for up to one week.

CHEESE & TOMATO
Bites

Serve these cheese-filled tomato cookies with pre-dinner drinks. Or why not pack a few into your lunchbox as a savory snack at any time of day?

MAKES: **30**
BAKING TIME: **10–12 MINUTES**

INGREDIENTS
1¼ cups all-purpose flour
½ teaspoon baking powder
6 tablespoons/¾ stick butter
1 teaspoon celery salt (optional)
2 tablespoons ketchup
FILLING
Scant ½ cup cream cheese
1 tablespoon snipped chives
Salt and freshly ground black pepper

1. Preheat the oven to 400°F. Lightly grease two baking sheets.

2. Place the flour and baking powder in a bowl. Blend in the butter until the mixture resembles fine bread crumbs. Stir in the celery salt, then add the ketchup and mix to form a stiff dough.

3. Roll out on a lightly floured counter and cut into 1-inch wafers with a knife or cookie cutter. Arrange on the baking sheets. Bake until golden, 10–12 minutes. Let cool on the baking sheets for a few minutes before transferring to a wire rack to cool completely.

4. Beat together the cream cheese and chives and season to taste. Use to sandwich two wafers together. The wafers will keep unfilled for up to one week in an airtight container; fill just prior to serving.

BLUE CHEESE & POPPYSEED Cookies

Great in a lunchbox these tasty cookies also make delightful cocktail snacks.

MAKES: 25–30
BAKING TIME: 10 MINUTES

INGREDIENTS
$1\frac{1}{3}$ cups all-purpose flour
Scant $\frac{1}{2}$ cup butter at room
  temperature
$\frac{1}{3}$ cup mild full-fat soft blue cheese
2 tablespoons poppyseeds

1. Put the flour, butter, and blue cheese into a bowl and mix well together. Place the mixture on plastic wrap and shape into a cylinder $1\frac{1}{2}$ inches in diameter. Chill until firm.

2. Preheat the oven to 350°F. Unwrap the dough and roll in the poppyseeds. Cut into slices and place $1\frac{1}{4}$ inches apart on a nonstick baking sheet. Bake for about 10 minutes until lightly browned. Cool on a wire rack.

COOKIE TIP
Always chill cookie dough in the refrigerator when instructed to do so. This will make the dough easier to work with when you are cutting into slices ready to bake.

OAT Cakes

The oaty flavor and texture of these savory
treats works very well with cheese and chutney.

MAKES: 12
BAKING TIME: 15–20 MINUTES

INGREDIENTS
1 cup fine oatmeal
Generous ⅓ cup all-purpose flour
1 teaspoon baking soda
1 teaspoon sugar
Pinch of salt
¼ cup/½ stick butter
1–2 tablespoons water

1. Preheat the oven to 350°F. Lightly grease a baking sheet.

2. Put the oatmeal, flour, baking soda, sugar, and salt in a mixing bowl. Place the butter and 1–2 tablespoons water in a small pan and heat until the butter melts. Stir into the oatmeal mixture and combine to form a dough.

3. Turn out onto a lightly floured counter and knead until the dough is no longer sticky, adding a little extra flour if necessary.

4. Roll out the dough until ⅛ inch thick and cut out 3-inch circles with a cookie cutter. Arrange on the baking sheet and bake until golden, 15–20 minutes. Remove to a wire rack to cool. Store in an airtight container for up to two weeks.

CHEWY TRAIL MIX Cookies

Healthy cookies that are truly delicious and will keep you going right till supper.

MAKES: 30
BAKING TIME: 20 MINUTES

INGREDIENTS

⅞ cup butter, softened
1 cup light brown sugar
¾ cup granulated sugar
4 tablespoons honey
2 eggs
2 teaspoons vanilla extract
3 cups all-purpose flour
½ teaspoon baking powder
½ teaspoon baking soda
1 teaspoon ground cinnamon
¼ teaspoon salt
¾ cup unsalted cashew nuts, chopped
¾ cup coarsely chopped walnuts
1 cup pumpkin seeds
½ cup sunflower seeds
1⅓ cups rolled oats
2 cups seedless raisins

1. Preheat the oven to 300°F. Use nonstick baking sheets or line baking sheets with parchment paper.

2. Put the butter, sugars, honey, eggs, and vanilla into a large bowl and beat well together. Sift together the flour, baking powder, baking soda, cinnamon, and salt. Mix into the butter mixture.

3. Stir in the cashews, walnuts, half the pumpkin seeds, sunflower seeds, oats, and raisins. Take pieces of dough about the size of an apricot and roll into balls. Dip one side into the reserved pumpkin seeds, place on the baking sheet and flatten with the palm of your hand.

4. Bake in the oven for 20 minutes. Allow to cool slightly on the baking sheet before removing to a wire rack.

COOKIE TIP
Honey is a great pantry standby and will last with the lid screwed tightly for quite a while. However, if it has crystallized over time, stand the jar in a pan of hot water until it liquifies again.

CHEESY
Crumbles

These chewy, cheesy bites are
the perfect bite-size snack.

MAKES: **20**
BAKING TIME: **15 MINUTES**

INGREDIENTS
4 ounces Monterey Jack or cheddar
  cheese
4 scallions
¼ cup walnuts
¾ cup all-purpose flour
1 teaspoon wholegrain Dijon mustard
6 tablespoons/¾ stick butter

1. Preheat the oven to 375°F. Grate the cheese coarsely into a bowl. Thinly slice the scallions and finely chop the walnuts and stir into the cheese. Stir in the flour and mustard.

2. Melt the butter and add to the cheese mixture, stirring until well blended. Shape into 1-inch balls and place on lightly greased baking sheets. Flatten slightly with a spatula.

3. Bake for about 15 minutes until golden brown. Leave to cool on the sheets for 2–3 minutes before transferring to a wire rack to cool completely. Best eaten warm or on the day they are made, but they can be stored in an airtight container in a cool place for up to three days.

BUTTER Cookies

Although this recipe for rough puff pastry is ideal for topping savory meat pies, it also makes fabulous cookies.

MAKES: 10-12
BAKING TIME: 8–10 MINUTES

INGREDIENTS
2 cups all-purpose flour
$1/2$ teaspoon salt
1 teaspoon baking powder
Pinch of baking soda
$3/4$ cup/$1^1/2$ sticks unsalted butter
6 tablespoons cold buttermilk
1 tablespoon melted butter, for
   brushing

COOKIE TIP
The dough can be made ahead and refrigerated or frozen and then baked fresh to eat with soup, or for breakfast or with roast meat and gravy.

1. Sift the flour, salt, baking powder, and baking soda into a mixing bowl. Cut the butter into dice, add to the flour, and blend together, using your fingertips until the mixture resembles coarse bread crumbs.

2. Stir in half the buttermilk and begin mixing the dough together, adding just enough of the remaining buttermilk to make a soft dough. Turn the dough onto a floured counter and dust with flour. Roll the dough out to 1 inch thick. Lift the dough from the counter and fold it in thirds. Give the dough a quarter turn. Flour the counter and dough again and reroll into a rectangle, of the same thickness. Repeat the folding and turning.

3. Transfer the dough to a baking sheet lined with parchment paper. Cover with plastic wrap and chill, about 20 minutes.

4. Remove from the refrigerator and repeat the rolling and folding twice more. Roll a final time to a $3/4$-inch thick rectangle. Now either cut the dough into triangles or use a cookie cutter to cut the dough into rounds.

5. Put the cut dough about 1 inch apart on the paper-lined baking sheet. Cover with plastic wrap and chill for at least 20 minutes.

6. Preheat the oven to 475°F. Brush the tops of the cookies with melted butter and transfer to the oven. Reduce the temperature to 375°F.

7. Bake until golden all over, 12–15 minutes. Let cool 5 minutes.

PIZZA Chunks

Although the ingredients may seem a little grown-up, these tasty crackers are a firm favorite with children.

MAKES: 24–30
BAKING TIME: 10–15 MINUTES

INGREDIENTS

1½ cups all-purpose flour
⅔ cup butter
¼ cup grated Parmesan cheese
¼ cup grated sharp cheddar cheese
1 tablespoon sun-dried tomato paste
1 ounce sun-dried tomatoes, coarsely chopped
1–2 teaspoons Italian dried mixed herbs
1 egg yolk
1 tablespoon water

1. Preheat the oven to 350°F. Put all the ingredients into a food processor and process, using the pulse button until the mixture just comes together.

2. Roll out the dough between sheets of parchment paper, to a large rectangle shape.

3. Remove the top piece of parchment paper and lift the dough, using the bottom paper, onto a baking sheet. Leave the bottom paper in place.
Using a fork or pastry wheel, mark lightly into squares or bars.

4. Bake in the oven for about 10–15 minutes until lightly browned.

5. Cool on a wire rack on the parchment paper and then break into pieces along the perforations.

COOKIE TIP
Always pay special attention when measuring flour for baking recipes—too much and your cookies will be too hard, and too little and your cookies will be flat.

KIDS'
COOKIES

GIANT M&M

Bites

These fun, giant cookies are perfect for packing in kids' lunchboxes, as a special treat.

MAKES: 12
BAKING TIME: 8–10 MINUTES

INGREDIENTS

½ cup/1 stick butter, softened

⅓ cup sugar

⅜ cup light brown sugar, firmly packed

1 egg

1 teaspoon vanilla extract

Scant 1⅓ cups self-rising flour

1 cup peanut or chocolate M&Ms or candy-coated chocolates

1. Preheat the oven to 375°F. Lightly grease two baking sheets.

2. Cream the butter and sugars together until light and fluffy. Beat in the egg and vanilla. Sift the flour and beat into the mixture. Add the M&Ms and stir until well combined.

3. Drop rounded tablespoons of the dough onto the baking sheets, spacing well apart as the cookies will almost double in size.

4. Bake until golden, 8–10 minutes. Let cool on the baking sheets for a few minutes before transferring to a wire rack to cool completely. These are best eaten the day they are made.

COOKIE TIP
Always stir flour prior to measuring—flour settles as it sits and if you don't stir it you may end up adding too much to your cookies.

PEANUT BUTTER
Cookies

If you prefer a soft, chewy cookie, bake only until the edges have browned slightly.

1. Preheat the oven to 350°F. Lightly grease two baking sheets.

2. Cream the butter and sugar together until pale and fluffy. Add the peanut butter, egg, and corn syrup and beat until well combined.

3. Sift the flour with the baking powder and work into the mixture to form a soft dough. On a lightly floured counter, knead the dough lightly, then shape into a thick log. Cover with plastic wrap and let chill for 30 minutes.

4. Cut the dough into slices ¼ inch thick and space well apart on the baking sheets. Press a crisscross pattern into the dough with the tines of a fork.

5. Bake until golden, 10–12 minutes. Let cool on the baking sheets for 2–3 minutes, then transfer to a wire rack to cool completely. Store in an airtight container for up to five days.

MAKES: **24**
BAKING TIME: **10–12 MINUTES**

INGREDIENTS
6 tablespoons/³/₄ stick butter
6 tablespoons sugar
½ cup crunchy peanut butter
1 egg
3 tablespoons light corn syrup
1¼ cups all-purpose flour
1 teaspoon baking powder

COOKIE TIP
Use smooth peanut butter if you prefer a creamier texture.

TEDDIES ON a Stick

Younger children will love these cute teddies
and they are great to make for cake sales.

MAKES: 25
BAKING TIME: 8–10 MINUTES

INGREDIENTS

LIGHT DOUGH
1$\frac{1}{2}$ cups all-purpose flour
$\frac{1}{2}$ teaspoon ground cinnamon
$\frac{1}{4}$ teaspoon baking soda
$\frac{1}{4}$ cup/$\frac{1}{2}$ stick butter
$\frac{1}{2}$ cup light brown sugar
2 tablespoons corn syrup
1 egg, beaten

DARK DOUGH
1$\frac{1}{2}$ cups all-purpose flour
$\frac{1}{2}$ teaspoon ground ginger
$\frac{1}{4}$ teaspoon baking soda
$\frac{1}{4}$ cup/1$\frac{1}{2}$ stick butter
$\frac{1}{2}$ cup dark brown sugar
2 tablespoons molasses
1 egg, beaten

TO SERVE
Wooden popsicle sticks
Semisweet and white chocolate chips

1. Preheat the oven to 375°F. Make up the dark and light dough in the same way.

2. Sift the flour, spice, and baking soda into a bowl. Blend in the butter and stir in the sugar. Warm the syrup or molasses in a small pan and add with the beaten egg to the flour mixture. Knead until smooth.

3. Roll out on a lightly floured counter and using a plain round 2$\frac{1}{2}$-inch cutter stamp out circles from the light and dark dough. Place on baking sheets lined with parchment paper. Insert a popsicle stick into the base of each circle.

4. Roll out the trimmings from each dough and using a plain round 1-inch cutter stamp out two rounds for each cookie. Use light dough with dark face and vice versa. Place one round on each cookie for the nose. Cut the other in half and place on the face for the ears. Mark the nose with a knife.

5. Bake in the oven for 8–10 minutes. Remove and while still warm position the chocolate chips for eyes.

TUTTI FRUTTI
Cookies

Packed full of fruit, these sweet cookies
are adored by young and old alike.

MAKES: 24
BAKING TIME: 10–12 MINUTES

INGREDIENTS

$^1/_2$ cup/1 stick butter, softened

Scant $^1/_2$ cup sugar

1 egg, lightly beaten

Grated zest and juice of $^1/_2$ orange

Generous 1$^1/_2$ cups all-purpose flour

Generous $^1/_4$ cup candied peel,
   chopped

Scant $^1/_2$ cup candied cherries,
   quartered

$^1/_4$ cup candied pineapple, chopped

1. Preheat the oven to 375°F. Lightly grease two baking sheets.

2. Cream the butter and sugar together until light and fluffy. Beat in the egg, orange juice, and zest. Add the flour and beat into the mixture. Stir in the fruit.

3. Drop rounded tablespoons of the dough onto the baking sheets, spacing well apart as the cookies will almost double in size.

4. Bake until golden, 10–12 minutes. Let cool on the baking sheets for a few minutes before transferring to a wire rack to cool completely

COOKIE TIP
When making drop cookies, use a spoon from your daily cutlery—not a measuring spoon—to drop them. The deep bowl of a measuring spoon will make the dough harder to remove.

CHOCOLATE & VANILLA Whirls

For these cookies, the dough should be quite soft; you may find it easier to handle if you roll it out on nonstick parchment paper. If it is too soft to roll, let chill for 10–15 minutes to firm slightly.

MAKES: 30
BAKING TIME: 10–12 MINUTES

INGREDIENTS

¾ cup/1½ sticks butter
¾ cup confectioners' sugar
1 teaspoon vanilla extract
Scant 1½ cups all-purpose flour
2 tablespoons chocolate hazelnut spread, such as Nutella
1 tablespoon unsweetened cocoa powder

1. Preheat the oven to 325°F. Lightly grease two baking sheets.

2. Cream the butter and confectioners' sugar together until pale and fluffy. Beat in the vanilla.

3. Add the flour into the mixture and blend to form a soft dough. Divide the dough in half and work the chocolate hazelnut spread and cocoa powder into one half.

4. Roll each piece of dough on a lightly floured counter to a 6 x 8-inch rectangle. Place one piece of dough on top of the other and press together lightly. Trim the edges and roll up lengthwise like a jelly roll. Cover and chill for 30 minutes.

5. Cut the dough into ¼-inch slices and space well apart on the baking sheets. Bake until golden, 10–12 minutes. Let cool 2–3 minutes on the baking sheets, then transfer to a wire rack to cool completely.

ICE CREAM SANDWICH Cookies

Great to make in the school vacation—either keep the cookies in an airtight container and make fresh sandwiches each time with softened ice cream or make the sandwiches complete with ice cream and freeze.

MAKES: 10
BAKING TIME: 15 MINUTES

INGREDIENTS
½ cup/1 stick unsalted butter at room temperature
½ cup superfine sugar
1 egg, beaten
1¾ cups all-purpose flour
¼ cup unsweetened cocoa powder, sifted
⅔ cup semisweet chocolate chips
Chocolate or vanilla ice cream

1. Preheat the oven to 350°F. Line a baking sheet with parchment paper.

2. Cream the butter and sugar together and beat in the egg. Stir in the flour, cocoa, and chocolate chips to make a firm dough. Roll out on nonstick parchment paper. Cut into 20 rectangles each 3 x 2½ inches.

3. Place on the baking sheet. Bake in the oven for about 15 minutes. Cool.

4. To make the ice cream cookies spread two good spoonfuls of softened ice cream on a cookie and press a second cookie on top. Squeeze so the filling reaches the edges. Eat straightaway or wrap individually in foil and freeze. May be kept up to two weeks in the freezer.

COOKIE TIP
You can use any flavor of ice cream for these sweet treats: choc chip, coconut, raspberry swirl, praline etc.

DOMINO Cookies

Make chocolate-flavored dominoes by substituting 2 tablespoons unsweetened cocoa powder for the same amount of flour. Pipe dots and lines with white frosting.

MAKES: 14
BAKING TIME: 8–10 MINUTES

INGREDIENTS
6 tablespoons/¾ stick butter,
    softened
⅓ cup sugar
1 egg
1 teaspoon vanilla extract
Scant 1½ cups all-purpose flour
¼ cup ground rice
1 ounce semisweet chocolate for
    decoration

1. Cream the butter and sugar together until light and fluffy. Beat in the egg and vanilla. Sift the flour and ground rice together and beat in to form a soft dough. Let chill for 30 minutes.

2. Preheat the oven to 350°F. Lightly grease a baking sheet. Roll out the dough on a lightly floured counter to about ¼ inch thick and cut out rectangles measuring about 2 x 3 inches. Arrange slightly spaced on the baking sheet.

3. Bake until pale golden, 10–12 minutes. Let cool on the baking sheet for a few minutes before transferring to a wire rack to cool completely.

4. To decorate, melt the chocolate in a microwave or in a bowl set over a pan of hot water. Spoon into a pastry bag fitted with a small writing tip. Pipe domino dots and lines onto the cookies and let set.

5. Store in an airtight container for up to one week.

NEAPOLITAN
Cookies

Children love making these simple but fun multicolored cookies.

MAKES: 24
BAKING TIME: 8–10 MINUTES

INGREDIENTS
¾ cup/1½ sticks butter, softened
⅔ cup sugar
1 teaspoon vanilla extract
Generous 1⅔ cups all-purpose flour
1 tablespoon unsweetened cocoa
   powder
1 teaspoon milk
½ teaspoon strawberry flavoring
Few drops red food coloring
   (optional)

COOKIE TIP
*If you only have
one baking sheet, make
sure you cool it well
between batches.*

1. Preheat the oven to 375°F. Lightly grease two baking sheets.

2. Cream the butter and sugar together until pale and fluffy. Beat in the vanilla. Add the flour and mix to form a smooth, soft dough. Divide into three equal portions.

3. Beat the cocoa powder and milk into one portion and mix to a smooth dough. Mix the strawberry flavoring and red food coloring, if using, into another portion. Leave the third portion plain.

4. Shape the chocolate-flavored portion into a sausage, then flatten to form a 2 x 10-inch rectangle. Repeat with the plain portion and place on top of the chocolate portion. Finally, repeat with the strawberry portion and stack on top.

5. Cut the bar into about 24 slices and lay flat on the baking sheets, allowing room for the cookies to spread. Bake until just firm, 8–10 minutes. Let cool on the baking sheets for a few minutes before transferring to a wire rack to cool completely.

MERINGUE Critters

Older kids can have fun making these meringue treats while younger ones can help Mum and eat the results!

MAKES: 14–16
BAKING TIME: 45–60 MINUTES

INGREDIENTS
2 egg whites
½ cup superfine sugar
FOR DECORATION
Confectioners' sugar
Licorice
Flaked almonds
Colored sugar sprinkles
Assorted candies for decoration

COOKIE TIP
When making meringue it is easier to separate the eggs when they are cold— but let the whites come to room temperature before using.

1. Put the egg whites in a bowl and beat until they form firm peaks. Gradually beat in the sugar a spoonful at a time. Beat for 15 seconds after each addition. Continue beating until very thick and shiny.

2. Preheat the oven to 300°F. Line a baking sheet with parchment paper.

3. Pipe critters as described below and bake in the oven for 45–60 minutes until dry and crisp.

Mice Spoon meringue into a pastry bag fitted with a 1-inch plain tip. Pipe a blob ½ inch high. Then pipe over this to make a shape like a mouse, taking pressure off the bag at the end to make a pointed nose. Place two silver balls or tiny pieces of candy for the eyes, and a licorice tail.

Hedgehogs Spoon meringue into a pastry bag fitted with a 1-inch fluted star tip and pipe as above. Add on eyes and place flaked almonds in the back for the spines.

Snails Spoon the meringue into a pastry bag fitted with a ½-inch plain tip. Pipe a small blob for the head and then pipe a spiral for the snail shell. Make feelers and eyes from pieces of candy or licorice.

Snakes Fill a pastry bag as for snails and pipe wavy lines about 5 inches long. Bake and allow to cool. When cold, glaze the meringue with a little confectioners' sugar and water and sprinkle with colored sugar sprinkles.

ICEBOX SUGAR
Cookies

The chill-and-bake nature of these cookies means that you can make the dough well ahead of time and bake the cookies as you need them.

1. Cream the butter and sugar together until pale and fluffy. Beat in the egg and vanilla. Add the flour and mix to form a soft dough.

2. Shape into a log about 2 inches thick. Spread the sugar sprinkles on a sheet of nonstick parchment paper and roll the log in the sugar until well coated.

3. Wrap the log in another sheet of parchment paper and chill until firm. At this point the dough can be stored in the refrigerator for up to one week, or placed in a plastic bag and frozen for up to two months.

4. When ready to bake, preheat the oven to 375°F. Lightly grease two baking sheets. Cut the log into slices $\frac{1}{8}$ inch thick and arrange carefully on the baking sheets, leaving enough room for the cookies to spread.

5. Bake until just firm, 8–10 minutes. Let cool on the baking sheets for a few minutes before transferring to a wire rack to cool completely.

MAKES: **45**
BAKING TIME: **8–10 MINUTES**

INGREDIENTS
$1\frac{1}{4}$ cups/$2\frac{1}{2}$ sticks butter, softened
Scant 1 cup sugar
1 egg
1 teaspoon vanilla extract
$2\frac{1}{3}$ cups all-purpose flour
Colored sugar sprinkles for decoration

COOKIE TIP
Preheat the oven for at least 10 minutes prior to baking.

ICED SPRINKLE
Cookies

Fun and colorful, you could also decorate these cookies with melted chocolate instead of the frosting. Use chocolate sprinkles, too.

MAKES: 18–24
BAKING TIME: 8 MINUTES

INGREDIENTS
½ cup/1 stick butter, softened
Scant ½ cup confectioners' sugar
1 teaspoon vanilla extract
1¼ cups all-purpose flour
2 tablespoons ground rice
FROSTING
Scant 1 cup confectioners' sugar
1 tablespoon water or lemon juice
Colored sugar sprinkles

1. Preheat the oven to 400°F.

2. Cream the butter and the confectioners' sugar together until pale and fluffy. Beat in the vanilla. Add the flour and ground rice and mix to form a soft dough.

3. Place the dough between two sheets of plastic wrap and roll out to about ⅛ inch thick. Cut out cookies using a 2–3-inch cookie cutter and carefully transfer to the baking sheets.

4. Bake until crisp and golden, about 8 minutes. Let cool on the baking sheets for a few minutes before transferring to a wire rack to cool completely.

5. Sift the confectioners' sugar into a bowl and add enough water or lemon juice to mix to a smooth frosting. Spread the frosting over the cookies with a metal spatula and decorate with sugar sprinkles. Let frosting set before serving.

COOKIE TIP
Always sift confectioners' sugar prior to use to avoid clumping.

ROCKY ROAD Cookies

Rich cookies, with a strong coconut taste. Decorate them by dipping in chocolate or drizzling a little chocolate over the top.

MAKES: 20
BAKING TIME: 12 MINUTES

INGREDIENTS
Generous 1½ cups all-purpose flour
1 teaspoon baking powder
½ cup/1 stick butter
Scant ½ cup sugar
1 egg
½ teaspoon vanilla extract
TOPPING
1 cup mini-marshmallows
Scant ⅔ cup chopped walnuts
2 ounces semisweet chocolate

1. Preheat the oven to 350°F. Lightly grease two baking sheets.

2. Sift the flour and baking powder together into a mixing bowl. In a separate bowl, cream the butter and sugar together until pale and fluffy. Beat in the egg and vanilla, then work in the flour mixture to form a soft dough.

3. Take small amounts of the dough, each about the size of a walnut, and roll into balls. Space well apart on the baking sheets and flatten slightly. Bake until just golden, about 12 minutes. Reduce the oven temperature to 325°F.

4. To make the topping: mix together the marshmallows and nuts. Melt the chocolate in a bowl set over a pan of gently simmering water, making sure the base of the bowl is not touching the water. Spread a little on top of each cookie and top with the marshmallow and nut mixture.

5. Return the cookies to the oven and bake 1–2 minutes until the marshmallow softens. Let cool on the baking sheets for 2–3 minutes before transferring to a wire rack to cool completely.

6. Drizzle or pipe the remaining chocolate over the cookies.

WHITE CHOCOLATE & CHERRY Cookies

Make up a batch of these scrumptious cookies for when only something sweet will do. Just try not to eat them all at once as they're utterly irresistible!

MAKES: 18
BAKING TIME: 12–15 MINUTES

INGREDIENTS
4 ounces white chocolate
$\frac{1}{2}$ cup/1 stick unsalted butter, softened
$\frac{1}{2}$ cup superfine sugar
1 egg
$1\frac{1}{4}$ cups rolled oats
$1\frac{1}{4}$ cups all-purpose flour
$\frac{1}{2}$ teaspoon baking powder
$\frac{1}{2}$ cup dried cherries

1. Preheat the oven to 350°F and grease two baking sheets. Chop the white chocolate into small chunks and set aside. Cream the butter and sugar together in a bowl until pale and fluffy. Beat in the egg, and then add the oats.

2. Sift the flour and baking powder over the mixture, and fold in. Stir in the white chocolate and cherries.

3. Drop dessertspoonfuls of the mixture onto the baking sheets, spacing them well apart. Flatten each one slightly and bake for 12–15 minutes, or until golden. Transfer to a wire rack to cool.

COOKIE TIP
Don't drop cookie dough onto a hot baking sheet as the cookies will spread too much.

CHOCOLATE THUMBPRINT Cookies

Kids love helping to bake these chocolate cookies. Using white chocolate to fill the well in each cookie gives a lovely color contrast. Alternatively, try using peanut butter for a smooth, nutty flavor.

Seedless Raspberry Preserves

MAKES: 24
BAKING TIME: 10 MINUTES

INGREDIENTS
2 ounces semisweet chocolate
4 tablespoons/1/2 stick butter
1/4 cup white vegetable shortening
Scant 1/4 cup sugar
1 1/4 cups all-purpose flour

FILLING
3 ounces semisweet, milk, or white
   chocolate

1. Melt the chocolate in a microwave or in a bowl set over a pan of hot water. Let cool.

2. Cream the butter, shortening, and sugar together until light and fluffy. Beat in the melted chocolate, then the flour and mix to form a smooth dough. Let chill for 30 minutes.

3. Preheat the oven to 350°F. Lightly grease a baking sheet. Shape the dough into 1-inch balls and arrange well spaced on the baking sheet. Press your thumb into the center of each ball to form a well.

4. Bake for 10 minutes. Let cool for a few minutes on the baking sheet, then transfer to a wire rack to cool completely.

5. For the filling, melt the chocolate in a microwave or in a bowl set over a pan of hot water. Spoon or pipe into the center of the cookies and let set.

SMILIES

Kids will love to make these cookies and they can show off their creative talents by making many different faces.

MAKES: 16
BAKING TIME: 8–10 MINUTES

INGREDIENTS
VANILLA MIX
1/2 cup/1 stick butter
1/4 cup superfine sugar
1 1/4 cups all-purpose flour
CHOCOLATE MIX
1/2 cup/1 stick butter
1/4 cup superfine sugar
1 1/8 cups all-purpose flour
2 tablespoons unsweetened cocoa powder
2 tablespoons drinking chocolate

1. Preheat the oven to 350°F. For each flavor cream together the butter and sugar until light and fluffy. Gradually mix in the remaining ingredients until a soft dough is formed.

2. Roll out the vanilla mixture on a lightly floured board to 1/4 inch thick. Using a 3-inch plain cutter stamp out biscuit faces. Place on a nonstick or lightly greased baking sheet. Keep the trimmings.

3. Roll out the chocolate mixture in the same way and cut out mouths, eyes, noses and hair and gently place on the vanilla faces. Curve the mouths up for smiles—maybe one turned down for sad.

4. Then cut out chocolate faces and use vanilla trimmings for the features.

5. Bake in the oven for about 10–12 minutes.

COOKIE TIP
Dip cutters in flour as you go along to keep the dough from sticking to them and tearing the cookies. Reroll as little as possible.

SNOWBALLS

Easy to make and very tasty to eat, these make a great Christmas gift.

MAKES: 12

INGREDIENTS

7 ounces white chocolate
2 tablespoons/¼ stick butter
1 cup sweetened and tenderized
  coconut
3½ ounces leftover sponge cake,
  crumbled
confectioners' sugar

1. Break the chocolate into pieces and place in a bowl with the butter. Put over a pan of gently simmering water.

2. Put ½ cup of the coconut onto a plate. Put the remaining coconut into a bowl with the crumbled cake crumbs. Add the melted chocolate and mix to form a paste.

3. Work quite quickly while the mixture is still warm. Roll the mixture into balls about the size of a walnut and immediately roll in the reserved coconut.

4. Leave to set and then dredge liberally with confectioners' sugar.

COOKIE TIP
Most confectioners' sugar, also known as powdered sugar, is blended with a small amount of cornstarch to prevent major lumping. Even so, it's usually best to sift it prior to use.

HOLIDAY
COOKIES

SWEETHEART
Cookies

These pretty cookies make a delightful gift for a friend or relative. Why not present them in a small basket or giftbox?

MAKES: 8
BAKING TIME: 15–20 MINUTES

INGREDIENTS
1 cup/2 sticks butter
Generous ½ cup confectioners' sugar
1 teaspoon vanilla extract
Scant ¼ cup cornstarch
Generous 1½ cups all-purpose flour
5 ounces semisweet chocolate

1. Preheat the oven to 350°F. Draw four heart shapes on two pieces of nonstick parchment paper. Place ink-side down on two baking sheets.

2. Cream the butter and confectioners' sugar together until pale and fluffy. Beat in the vanilla. Sift together the cornstarch and flour, and beat into the mixture.

3. Place the dough in a large pastry bag fitted with a star tip. Pipe heart shapes onto the parchment paper following the line drawings.

4. Bake until pale gold, 15–20 minutes. Let cool on the baking sheets for 2–3 minutes, then transfer to a wire rack to cool completely.

5. Melt the chocolate in a bowl set over a pan of gently simmering water. Let cool slightly, then dip half of each heart in the chocolate to decorate. Store in an airtight container for up to four days.

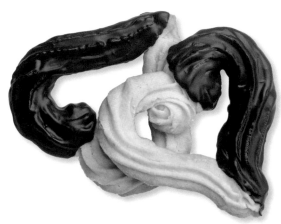

LIPSMACKING KISS Cookies

The perfect Valentine's Day gift for that special someone.

1. Preheat the oven to 400°F. Draw a lip shape onto a piece of card, cut out, and set aside to use as a template.

2. Blend the butter into the flour until the mixture resembles fine bread crumbs. Stir in the sugar, egg, and 1–2 tablespoons cold water to bind the mixture to a soft but not sticky dough. Chill for 20 minutes.

3. Roll out on a lightly floured counter to a ¼-inch thickness. Using the template, cut around it to make 20 kiss cookies. Space well apart on two baking sheets and bake for 7–8 minutes. Allow to cool completely.

4. Roll out the fondant on a surface lightly dusted with confectioners' sugar to a ⅛-inch thickness and cut out 20 kisses using the template.

5. Sift the confectioners' sugar and mix with 2 teaspoons water to a very thick paste. Add a little red food coloring to make a smooth, thick, pink glacé icing. Spoon into a paper pastry bag and snip off the end. Pipe a few dots on each cookie. Lift the fondant kisses and place 1 on top of each cookie. Pipe a fine line of pink icing over each of the fondant kisses to define the outline. Leave to set.

MAKES: 20
BAKING TIME: 7–8 MINUTES

INGREDIENTS
½ cup/1 stick butter, cut into cubes
2 cups all-purpose flour
¾ cup sugar
1 egg, beaten
10 ounces red fondant icing
¾ cup confectioners' sugar
Red food coloring

COOKIE TIP
These cookies could be presented in a pretty giftbox with pretty tissue paper and ribbons.

STAINED GLASS CHRISTMAS Cookies

These cookies are really easy to make and yet look so impressive. They make great gifts for the festive season.

MAKES: 12
BAKING TIME: 14 MINUTES

INGREDIENTS

1 ½ cups all-purpose flour

⅓ cup butter

3 tablespoons superfine sugar

1 egg white

2 tablespoons orange juice

8 ounces hard candies in assorted colors

Thin ribbon or cord

COOKIE TIP
These cookies look wonderful when hung on the Christmas tree or beside candles, to catch the light.

1. Preheat the oven to 350°F. Line baking sheets with parchment paper.

2. Put the flour into a bowl and blend in the butter. Stir in the sugar, egg white, and enough orange juice to mix to a soft dough. Knead lightly.

3. Roll out the dough on a lightly floured counter and cut into shapes such as stars, hearts, flowers, Christmas trees etc. Cut out the centers of the cookies using a similar shaped cutter or a plain round cutter.

4. Make a hole on the top of the cookie with a skewer. Place on the prepared baking sheet and bake in the oven for 4 minutes. Remove and place a candy in the center of each cookie and return to the oven for an additional 10 minutes or until the cookies are golden brown and the candies have melted and filled the centers of the cookies.

5. Remove from the oven and put a skewer in the holes at the top of each cookies to open them up. Leave the cookies on the baking sheet until cool and set and then peel them off. Thread ribbon or cord through the holes at the top of each cookie.

SNOWFLAKE Cookies

Leave these cookies out for a late-night treat for Santa Claus.

MAKES: 20
BAKING TIME: 6–8 MINUTES

INGREDIENTS
1¼ cups all-purpose flour
½ cup/1 stick butter
1¼ cups confectioners' sugar
½ teaspoon ground cardamom
1 egg yolk
1 tablespoon milk
½ teaspoon vanilla extract
6 ounces white fondant
1 tablespoon sugar
Silver balls for decoration

1. Put the flour, butter, and half the confectioners' sugar into a mixing bowl or food processor and mix until it resembles fine bread crumbs. Add the ground cardamom, egg yolk, milk, and vanilla extract and mix until it forms a soft ball. Chill for 30 minutes.

2. Preheat the oven to 400°F. Roll out the dough on a lightly floured counter to ¼-inch thickness and cut out 20 cookies using a snowflake paper template. Evenly space apart on two baking sheets and bake for 6–8 minutes. Cool on the baking sheets for 10 minutes before transferring to a wire rack to cool completely.

3. Roll out the fondant on a surface lightly dusted with confectioners' sugar to ⅛-inch thickness and cut out 20 snowflakes the same size as the cookies.

4. Mix the remaining confectioners' sugar with 2 teaspoons water to a thick paste, spoon into a paper pastry bag and snip off the tip. Pipe small dots over the cookies and lift the fondant snowflakes on top, pressing down lightly to secure. Push the fondant in all around the shape to leave a small gap between the cookie and the fondant. Use the remaining glacé icing to pipe snowflake lines over the fondant icing. Sprinkle immediately with the sugar and decorate with the silver balls.

GINGERBREAD CHRISTMAS Cookies

To be able to hang the cookies make a hole at the top of each one before baking. Reopen the hole as soon as they come out of the oven.

MAKES: 30–40
BAKING TIME: 10–12 MINUTES

INGREDIENTS

2$\frac{1}{3}$ cups all-purpose flour

1 tablespoon baking powder

2 teaspoons ground ginger

$\frac{1}{2}$ teaspoon ground allspice

$\frac{1}{4}$ cup molasses

$\frac{1}{4}$ cup light corn syrup

6 tablespoons/$\frac{3}{4}$ stick butter

3 tablespoons dark brown sugar,
    firmly packed

1 egg, beaten

FROSTING

Scant 1$\frac{1}{4}$ cups confectioners' sugar

1 tablespoon lemon juice

1. Lightly grease two baking sheets. Sift the flour, baking powder, and spices together into a bowl.

2. Place the molasses, corn syrup, butter, and brown sugar in a small pan and heat gently, stirring until well combined.

3. Let cool slightly, then beat in the egg. Pour into the dry ingredients and mix to form a firm dough. Let rest for a few minutes, then knead gently until smooth.

4. Preheat the oven to 350°F. On a lightly floured counter roll out the dough to $\frac{1}{4}$ inch thick, and cut out cookies with cookie cutters. Place on the baking sheets and bake until crisp and golden, 10–12 minutes. Let cool on the baking sheets for 2–3 minutes, then transfer to a wire rack to cool completely.

5. To make the frosting, sift the confectioners' sugar into a bowl, add the lemon juice, and mix until smooth. Spread or pipe over the cookies. Let stand until the frosting has set, 1–2 hours. Store in an airtight container for up to two weeks.

SPECULAAS

A traditional Dutch cookie, these are eaten in Holland around the feast of St Nicholas, which is December 6. They are made from a spicy dough wrapped around a soft marzipan filling.

MAKES: 35
BAKING TIME: 35 MINUTES

INGREDIENTS

1$\frac{1}{2}$ cups hazelnuts, toasted and ground
1 cup ground almonds
$\frac{3}{4}$ cup superfine sugar
1$\frac{1}{2}$ cups confectioners' sugar
1 egg, beaten
2–3 teaspoons lemon juice
DOUGH
2$\frac{1}{4}$ cups self-rising flour
1 teaspoon pumpkin pie spice
$\frac{3}{8}$ cup brown sugar
$\frac{1}{2}$ cup unsalted butter
2 eggs
1 tablespoon milk
1 tablespoon superfine sugar
About 35 blanched almond halves

1. Put all the filling ingredients into a bowl and mix to a firm paste. Divide in half and roll each piece to a sausage shape about 10 inches long. Wrap in plastic wrap and chill while making the dough.

2. Sift the flour and spice into a bowl and stir in the sugar. Blend in the butter. Beat one of the eggs and add to the mixture and mix together to form a soft, but firm dough. Knead lightly and chill for 15 minutes.

3. Preheat the oven to 350°F. Line a baking sheet with parchment paper.

4. Roll out the dough to a 12-inch square and cut in half to make two strips. Beat the remaining egg and use to brush all over the pastry strips. Place a roll of filling on each strip and roll up like a sausage roll to completely enclose the filling. Place join side down on the prepared baking sheets.

5. Beat the remains of the egg with the milk and sugar and brush over the rolls. Decorate with halved almonds all along the top. Bake for about 35 minutes until golden brown. Allow to become cold before cutting diagonally into slices.

DEEP FRIED CHRISTMAS Cookies

In Norway these cookies are called reindeer antlers and are made at Christmas, but there are variations all over Europe variously known as "bits and pieces," "rags and tatters" and so on. It is best to make the dough the day before and leave in the refrigerator to firm up.

MAKES: 30

INGREDIENTS

2 egg yolks
$\frac{1}{4}$ cup superfine sugar
4 tablespoons heavy cream
1 tablespoon brandy
1 teaspoon ground cardamom
1 teaspoon finely grated lemon zest
$\frac{1}{4}$ cup/$\frac{1}{2}$ stick butter
$1\frac{3}{4}$ cups all-purpose flour
Vegetable oil for deep-frying
Sugar and cinnamon for dusting

1. Put the egg yolks and sugar into a bowl and whisk until thick and pale. Add the cream, brandy, cardamom, and lemon zest. Blend the butter into the flour. Add the egg mixture to the flour and mix to a soft dough. Cover in plastic wrap and leave in the refrigerator overnight.

2. The next day, roll out the dough on a lightly floured counter to $\frac{1}{4}$-inch thickness. Using a zigzag pastry wheel cut into strips $1\frac{1}{2}$ x 4 inches. Cut a slit 1 inch long lengthwise in the center of each rectangle. Pull one end of the strip through this slit to make a half bow shape.

3. Heat the oil until a cube of bread browns in 1 minute. Deep-fry the cookies a few at a time until golden brown. Remove with a slotted spoon and drain on paper towels. Dust liberally with mixed sugar and cinnamon.

RUSSIAN
Teacakes

These buttery sugar-dusted teacakes are often served at weddings. When made with pecans they are known as Mexican or Portuguese wedding cakes and when made with almonds they are the Greek version known as kourabiedes.

MAKES: 20
BAKING TIME: 15 MINUTES

INGREDIENTS
½ cup/1 stick unsalted butter
2 teaspoons orange flower water
½ cup confectioners' sugar
¾ cup all-purpose flour
1 cup lightly toasted ground walnuts
¼ cup lightly toasted walnut pieces, chopped
Confectioners' sugar for dusting

1. Preheat the oven to 350°F. Line baking sheets with parchment paper. Beat the butter until soft and creamy.

2. Beat in the orange flower water. Add the confectioners' sugar and beat until fluffy. Add the flour, ground and chopped walnuts and mix well using your hand to bring the mixture together. Don't over work the dough. Chill if the mixture is a little soft.

3. Either roll the mixture into balls or shape pieces of dough into sausages about 3 inches long. Curve each one into a crescent shape and place well apart on the prepared baking sheets.

4. Bake in the oven for about 15 minutes or until firm and still pale in color. Cool for about 5 minutes and then dredge liberally with confectioners' sugar.

PERSIAN RICE
Cookies

These pretty rose-scented cookies are traditionally offered at special occasions such as weddings.

MAKES: 20
BAKING TIME: 18–20 MINUTES

INGREDIENTS

DOUGH

²/₃ cup confectioners' sugar

1 cup/2 sticks very soft unsalted butter

2¹/₂ cups rice flour

²/₃ cup self-rising flour

1 egg yolk

1 tablespoon rose water

TOPPING

²/₃ cup sifted confectioners' sugar

Rose water

Pink food coloring (optional)

Crystallized rose petals for decoration

1. Put all the ingredients for the dough into a bowl and mix well together. Wrap in plastic wrap and chill until firm.

2. Preheat the oven to 350°F. Line baking sheets with parchment paper.

3. Shape the mixture into balls the size of large walnuts. Place well apart on the prepared baking sheets and flatten each one slightly.

4. Bake for 18–20 minutes until firm but still pale. Let cool completely on the sheets, as these cookies are extremely crumbly while hot.

5. To make the topping put the confectioners' sugar into a bowl and add just enough rose water to mix to a thick flowing consistency. If desired add a touch of pink coloring to make a very pale shade. Drizzle the icing over the cookies and decorate with crystallized rose petals.

COOKIE TIP
To prevent baking parchment slipping off baking sheets, sprinkle the sheet with a few drops of water beforehand.

EASTER Bonnets

These pretty, colorful cookies make wonderful easter gifts.

1. Cream the butter and sugar together until pale, beat in the egg and stir in the flour, baking powder, vanilla extract, orange zest, and a little of the orange juice to bind to a soft, pliable dough. Chill for 30 minutes.

2. Preheat the oven to 350°F. Roll out on a lightly floured counter to a $1/4$-inch thickness and cut out 18 circles with a $3^1/4$-inch round cutter. Space out the circles on two baking sheets and bake for 10–12 minutes. Cool on the baking sheets for 10 minutes before transferring to a wire rack to cool completely.

3. Pinch off small balls of fondant and roll out on a surface dusted with confectioners' sugar to an $1/8$-inch thickness. Cut out tiny flower shapes to decorate the bonnets and push a colored ball into the center of each. Color half the remaining fondant pink and half yellow and roll out to an $1/8$-inch thickness. Cut out nine circles measuring $3^1/4$ inches from each.

4. Warm the remaining orange juice and mix 2 tablespoons with the creamed coconut and confectioners' sugar to make a smooth paste. Spoon a teaspoonful of the mixture into the center of each cookie. Cover with the circles of colored fondant and press down lightly to shape the bonnet. Decorate with the ribbon and flowers, securing them with a little confectioners' sugar mixed with water.

MAKES: 18
BAKING TIME: 10–12 MINUTES

INGREDIENTS
$3/4$ cup/$1^1/2$ sticks butter
$3/4$ cup sugar
1 large egg, beaten
3 cups all-purpose flour
1 teaspoon. baking powder
1 teaspoon. vanilla extract
Finely grated zest and juice of 1 small orange
$1^1/4$ pounds white fondant
Red and yellow food coloring
Colored balls and ribbon for decoration
4 ounces creamed coconut
$1/2$ cup confectioners' sugar

EASTER
Cookies

These currant-filled cookies are traditionally baked for the Christian festival of Easter and in the past they would be eaten after church on Easter morning. They are tied with thin ribbon in bundles of three to represent the Trinity.

MAKES: 18
BAKING TIME: 15–20 MINUTES

INGREDIENTS
1^2/$_3$ cups all-purpose flour
^{1}/$_4$ cup rice flour
1 teaspoon mixed spice
^{1}/$_2$ cup/1 stick butter
^{1}/$_2$ cup superfine sugar
2 egg yolks
^{1}/$_3$ cup currants
1 tablespoon chopped mixed peel
1–2 tablespoons milk
1 egg white, very lightly beaten
Superfine sugar to sprinkle

1. Preheat the oven to 350°F. Use lightly greased or nonstick baking sheets.

2. Mix together the flour, rice flour, and mixed spice. In another bowl cream together the butter and sugar. Beat in the egg yolks and then add the currants and mixed peel. Stir in the flour with enough milk to mix to a fairly stiff dough.

3. Knead lightly and then roll out on a lightly floured counter to ^{1}/$_4$ inch thick. Using a 4-inch round fluted cutter cut out cookies and place on the baking sheets.

4. Bake in the oven for 10 minutes then remove from the oven. Brush with the egg white and sprinkle with superfine sugar. Return to the oven for a further 5–10 minutes until lightly browned. Place on a wire rack to cool.

MOTHER'S DAY
Handful Of Love

This is a lovely way to say "thank you" on Mother's Day. Each child can cut out the shape of their hand and decorate with frosting and candies or use purchased frosting in tubes and pipe a message on top.

MAKES: 4–6 HANDS DEPENDING ON SIZE
BAKING TIME: 10–15 MINUTES

INGREDIENTS
3 cups self-rising flour
2 teaspoons ground cinnamon
1/4 cup honey
1 cup brown sugar
1/4 cup/1/2 stick butter
1 egg, beaten
Finely grated zest of 1 lemon
1 tablespoon lemon juice
FOR DECORATION
Blanched almonds
Ready made frosting
Candies, silver balls etc.

1. Preheat the oven to 350°F. Line a baking sheet with parchment paper. Put each child's hand on a piece of thin card (cereal boxes are good) and draw around it. Cut out and use as templates.

2. Put the flour and cinnamon into a bowl and mix together.

3. Put the honey, sugar, and butter into a saucepan and heat very gently until melted. Cool slightly. Pour into the flour mixture and add the egg, lemon zest, and juice. Mix to form a soft dough. Knead lightly.

4. Roll out the dough on a lightly floured counter. Using the templates cut out hands from the dough and carefully place on the baking sheet. Reroll the trimmings and using a small heart-shaped cutter, stamp out a heart for each hand. Place a heart between the first finger and thumb of each hand. Press almonds in the fingers to represent fingernails. Bake in the oven for about 10–15 minutes depending on size.

5. When cold decorate as desired.

CHOCOLATE PUMPKIN Cookies

For this recipe you need a pumpkin-shaped cookie cutter or draw a pumpkin about 5–6 inches in diameter on some card and use as a stencil.

MAKES: **ABOUT 8, DEPENDING SIZE OF TEMPLATE**
BAKING TIME: **8–10 MINUTES**

INGREDIENTS
1½ cups all-purpose flour
¾ cup unsweetened cocoa powder
1 teaspoon ground cinnamon
¾ cup/1½ sticks unsalted butter
¾ cup superfine sugar
1 large egg, beaten
10 ounces ready to use fondant, colored orange
1–2 tablespoons honey, warmed

1. Sift together the flour, cocoa, and cinnamon. Put the butter and sugar into a bowl and beat until light and fluffy. Beat in the egg. Gradually stir in the flour mixture. Cover in plastic wrap and chill until firm.

2. Preheat the oven to 375°F. Line baking sheets with parchment paper. On a floured counter roll out the dough to ¼ inch thick. Using a cutter or the cardboard stencil and a sharp knife, cut out pumpkin shapes.

3. Carefully place on the baking sheets and bake for 8–10 minutes until crisp but not too browned. Leave to cool on a wire rack.

4. Trim the cardboard templates so they are slightly smaller all round. Roll out the fondant, and using the template, cut out one shape for each cookie.

5. Using the back of a knife mark grooves as on a pumpkin. Using a small pointed knife cut out eyes, nose, and mouth. Brush each cookie with a little warm honey and place a fondant face on each one. Leave to dry.

HALLOWE'EN TOFFEE APPLE Cookies

Great for those Trick or Treat bags at Hallowe'en these cookies are a mixture of chewy oats, soft apple, sweet raisin, and wonderfully crunchy toffee.

MAKES: 18
BAKING TIME: 12–15 MINUTES

INGREDIENTS

$2/3$ cup all-purpose flour
$1/2$ teaspoon baking soda
$1/2$ teaspoon ground cinnamon
$2/3$ cup unsalted butter
scant 1 cup brown sugar
$1/2$ cup sugar
1 large egg, beaten
$2 1/2$ cups rolled oats
Scant $1/2$ cup raisins
2 ounces ready-to-eat dried apple rings, roughly chopped
2 ounces chewy toffees, roughly cut up

1. Preheat the oven to 350°F. Line baking sheets with parchment paper. Sift together the flour, baking soda, and cinnamon.

2. Put the butter and both sugars into a bowl and beat together until creamy. Add the egg to the butter mixture and beat well. Add the flour mixture and mix thoroughly. Add the oats, raisins, apple, and toffee pieces and stir until just combined.

3. Using a small ice cream scoop or large tablespoon place dollops of mixture well apart onto the baking sheets. Bake in the oven for about 12–15 minutes depending on size, or until lightly set in the center and the edges are just beginning to turn brown,

4. Let cool on the sheets for a few minutes and do not touch as the melted toffee will be extremely hot and will set as the mixture cools down. Using a spatula place the cookies on a cooling rack to cool.

SKELETON Lollipops

These crisp, spiced cookies look very impressive. You will need to cut out a template in the shape of a skull to make these cookies.

1. Cream the butter and sugar together until pale, beat in the egg and stir in the flour, baking powder, and mixed spice. Stir in a little milk if necessary to bind to a soft, pliable dough. Chill for 30 minutes.

2. Preheat the oven to 350°F. Roll out on a floured counter to ¼-inch thickness and cut out 24 circles with a 3¼-inch cutter. Evenly space the circles apart on two baking sheets, slip a wooden popsicle stick 1 inch under each cookie and press down lightly. Bake for 10–12 minutes. Cool on the baking sheets for 10 minutes before transferring to a wire rack to cool completely.

3. Roll out the fondant on a surface lightly dusted with confectioners' sugar to ⅛-inch thickness. Using a skull paper template, cut out 24 skull shapes, rerolling the fondant if necessary.

4. Melt the chocolate in a microwave or a glass bowl set over a pan of simmering water. Spoon into a paper pastry bag and snip off the tip. If necessary, secure the popsicle sticks to the cookies with some of the melted chocolate and allow to set. Pipe small dots over the top half of the cookies and arrange the fondant skulls on top. Pipe the eyes and a nose onto each of the skulls, then paint on the mouth and teeth with the black food coloring.

MAKES: **24**
BAKING TIME: **10–12 MINUTES**

INGREDIENTS
¾ cup/1½ sticks butter
¾ cup sugar
1 egg, beaten
3 cups all-purpose flour
1 teaspoon baking powder
1 teaspoon mixed spice
Milk
12 ounces white fondant
24 flat wooden popsicle sticks
7 ounces semisweet chocolate
Black food coloring

BLUEBERRY SHORTCAKE Cookies

These cookies must be eaten on the day they are made and are especially good warm from the oven. You can substitute with small, halved strawberries or raspberries for a special 4th of July treat.

MAKES: 8
BAKING TIME: 20 MINUTES

INGREDIENTS
1¼ cups all-purpose flour
1½ teaspoons baking powder
¼ cup/½ stick unsalted butter
¼ cup granulated sugar
Finely grated zest of 1 lemon
½ cup sour cream
1 cup fresh blueberries
Crushed sugar cubes for sprinkling

1. Preheat the oven to 375°F. Line a baking sheet with parchment paper.

2. Sift the flour and baking powder into a bowl. Blend in the butter until the mixture resembles fine bread crumbs. Stir in the sugar and lemon zest.

3. Stir in the sour cream and blueberries and stir until just combined. Spo 8 mounds, well apart, on the prepared baking sheet. Sprinkle with the crushed sugar cubes and bake in the oven for about 20 minutes until golden and firm in the center. Serve warm and eat on the day of baking.

COOKIE TIP
Baked and uncooked shaped cookies can be frozen for up to two months. Thaw baked cookies at room temperature and bake uncooked ones from frozen.

RUGELACH

Little crescents made with a delicious cream cheese dough containing a spicy fruit and nut filling. These cookies are traditionally served during the eight-day Jewish festival of Hanukkah.

MAKES: 24–30
BAKING TIME: 15–20 MINUTES

INGREDIENTS

DOUGH
$\frac{1}{2}$ cup/1 stick unsalted butter, chilled
$\frac{1}{2}$ cup cream cheese
$\frac{1}{2}$ cup sour cream
2$\frac{1}{4}$ cups all-purpose flour

FILLING
$\frac{1}{4}$ cup superfine sugar
2 teaspoons ground cinnamon
4 tablespoons raisins, chopped
4 tablespoons ready-to-eat dried
   apricots, chopped
$\frac{3}{4}$ cup walnuts, finely chopped
Beaten egg for glazing

1. To make the dough put the butter, cream cheese, and sour cream into a food processor and blend until just creamy. Add the flour and blend very briefly, using the pulse button until the mixture just comes together. Remove and wrap in plastic wrap and chill overnight or at least 6 hours.

2. Preheat the oven to 350°F. Line baking sheets with parchment paper. Put the filling ingredients into a bowl and mix together.

3. Divide the dough into four. Take one piece and leave the rest in the refrigerator as it is important to keep the dough as cold as possible as it is very sticky to roll out. Sprinkle a sheet of parchment paper with flour, put the dough in the center and place another sheet of parchment paper on top. Quickly roll out the dough to a circle.

4. Cut into six wedges and sprinkle evenly with a quarter of the filling. Starting at the wide end, roll each triangle up toward the point. Curve each roll into a crescent and place with the pointed side down on the baking sheets. Repeat with the remaining dough.

5. Brush with beaten egg and bake in the oven for about 15–20 minutes or until golden brown. Cool on a wire rack.

CHINESE FORTUNE
Cookies

The messages in these cookies traditionally contain predictions of the future and are popular at the New Year.

MAKES: 35
BAKING TIME: 5 MINUTES

INGREDIENTS

2 egg whites
1/2 cup confectioners' sugar, sifted
1 teaspoon almond extract
2 tablespoons/1/2 stick unsalted
    butter, melted
1/2 cup all-purpose flour
1/3 cup unsweetened, shredded
    coconut, lightly toasted
Confectioners' sugar for sprinkling
Tiny strips of paper with good luck
    and other appropriate messages
    typed on them

1. Preheat the oven to 375°F. Prepare two or three sheets of parchment paper (they can be used more than once) by cutting them to the size of the baking sheet. Draw two or three circles of about 3 inches diameter on each sheet of paper. Place on the baking sheet.

2. Put the egg whites into a bowl and beat until soft peaks form. Beat in the confectioners' sugar a little at a time. Beat in the almond extract and butter. Stir in the flour and mix until smooth.

3. Place a teaspoonful of mixture in the center of a marked circle and spread out thinly and evenly to fit the circle. Sprinkle with a little coconut. Bake one sheet at a time, in the oven, for about 5 minutes or until very lightly brown on the edges.

4. Remove from the oven and immediately lift the cookies from the sheet and loosely fold in half tucking a message inside. Rest the cookie over the rim of a glass so the cookie bends in the center. Let cool and when firm remove to a cooling rack. Continue to bake and shape the remaining cookies in the same way. Sprinkle very lightly with confectioners' sugar.

CORN & CRANBERRY Cookies

These little cookies are not overly sweet and have a lovely hint of orange and the delightful addition of cranberry. They make an ideal accompaniment to midmorning or after-dinner coffee.

MAKES: 16
BAKING TIME: 8–10 MINUTES

INGREDIENTS

1/3 cup butter

3/4 cup fine cornmeal, plus extra for dusting

1 cup all-purpose flour

1/4 cup superfine sugar

1 egg

Finely grated zest of 1 orange

3/4 cup dried sweetened cranberries

1. Preheat the oven to 375°F.

2. Put the butter, cornmeal, and flour into a bowl. Blend in the butter. Stir in the sugar.

3. Add the egg, orange zest, and cranberries and mix well together with your hands until the mixture just comes together.

4. Shape into small sticks and roll in cornmeal. Place on nonstick baking sheets and bake in the oven for about 8–10 minutes until just beginning to brown.

COOKIE TIP
Only grease baking sheets when a recipe instructs you to. Otherwise the cookies may spread too much and become flat.

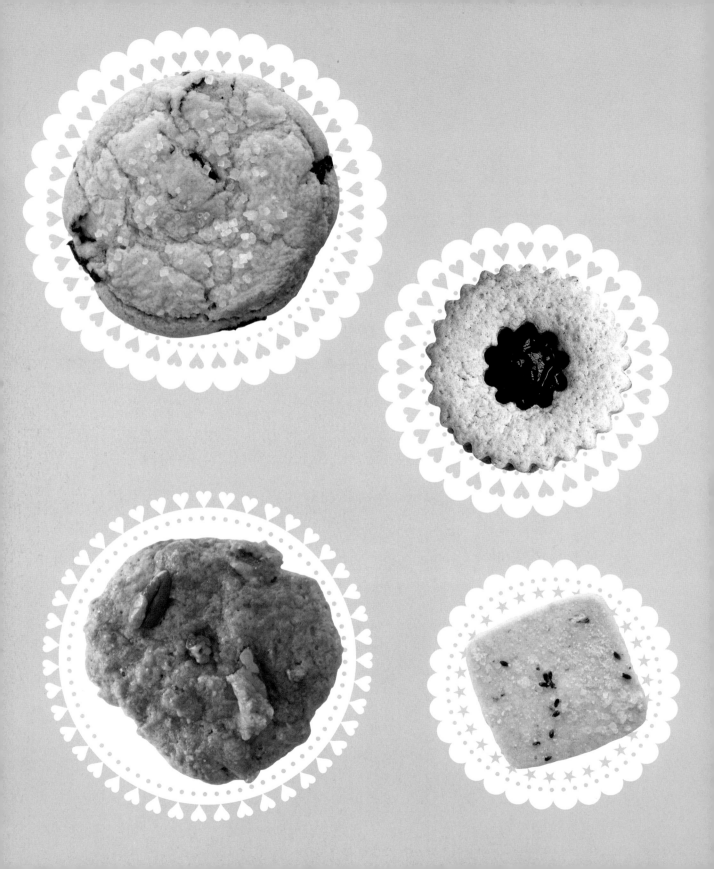

CHOCOLATE
CARAMEL Slices

These delicious marbled slices are
perfect for any special occasion.

MAKES: **12**
BAKING TIME: **25 MINUTES**

INGREDIENTS
½ cup butter, softened
¼ cup sugar
1 cup all-purpose flour
3 tablespoons cornstarch
FILLING
6 tablespoons butter
¼ cup packed light brown sugar
1 tablespoon light corn syrup
14oz canned sweetened condensed
   milk
TOPPING
4oz semi-sweet or milk chocolate
1 tablespoon butter
1oz white chocolate

1. Preheat the oven to 350°F. Grease an 8 x 8in square cake pan and line the base with non-stick baking parchment.

2. Cream the butter and sugar together until light and fluffy. Sift together the flour and cornstarch and mix in to form a smooth dough. Press the mixture into the base of the pan. Bake until just golden and firm, about 25 minutes.

3. To make the filling, combine the ingredients in a pan and heat gently, stirring until the sugar dissolves. Bring slowly to a boil and boil the mixture gently for about 5 minutes, stirring constantly with a wooden spoon until thickened. Pour evenly over the cookie base.

4. To make the topping, melt the semi-sweet or milk chocolate in a bowl set over a pan of hot water. Stir in the butter. Spread over the caramel filling. Melt the white chocolate in the same way. Spoon into a pastry bag and pipe squiggles over the darker chocolate. (Alternatively, drizzle the white chocolate from a spoon.) Swirl with a skewer to create a marbled effect and leave to set. Serve cut into squares.

GRANDMA'S
FAVORITES

Flat MAPLE GLAZED Cookies

These sticky cookies have a soft, chewy texture that children love.

MAKES: 18
BAKING TIME: 15 MINUTES

INGREDIENTS

1¼ cups all-purpose flour
1 teaspoon baking powder
½ teaspoon baking soda
6 tablespoons/¾ stick butter, cut into cubes
⅓ cup sugar
Scant ½ cup pecans, chopped *← More*
1 egg, lightly beaten
6 tablespoons maple syrup

Roll in balls

1. Preheat the oven to 350°F. Lightly grease two baking sheets.

2. Sift the flour, baking powder, and baking soda into a bowl. Add the butter and blend with your fingertips until the mixture resembles fine bread crumbs. Stir in the sugar and pecans.

3. Add the egg and 4 tablespoons of the maple syrup and mix until well combined.

4. Drop small heaping tablespoonfuls *- Smaller* of the dough, slightly spaced apart onto the baking sheets. Bake until golden, about 15 minutes.

5. Brush the cookies with the remaining maple syrup while still hot, then transfer to a wire rack to cool completely.

COOKIE TIP

Always pay special attention when measuring flour for baking recipes—too much and your cookies will be too hard and too little and they will turn out too flat.

SOUR CREAM & RAISIN Cookies

If your raisins are a bit dried out, plump them up by soaking in hot water for about 10 minutes. Rinse with cool water, squeeze dry, and coat lightly in flour from the recipe before adding to the dough.

MAKES: 18
BAKING TIME: 10–12 MINUTES

INGREDIENTS
½ cup/1 stick butter
⅔ cup sugar
6 tablespoons sour cream
1¼ cups all-purpose flour
1 teaspoon baking soda
Scant ½ cup raisins

1. Preheat the oven to 350°F. Lightly grease two baking sheets.

2. Cream the butter and sugar together until pale and fluffy. Beat in the sour cream.

3. Sift the flour and baking soda together, then beat into the mixture. Stir in the raisins.

4. Drop tablespoons of the dough well apart on the baking sheets. Bake until golden, 10–12 minutes. Let cool on the baking sheets for 2–3 minutes, then transfer to a wire rack to cool completely.

COOKIE TIP
Always allow cookies to cool completely before transferring to an airtight storage container.

SPICED MOLASSES
Cookies

Rich and spicy, these cookies are
delicious served with a cup of coffee.

MAKES: 10–12
BAKING TIME: 12–15 MINUTES

INGREDIENTS

1½ cups sifted all-purpose flour
2 teaspoons baking soda
¼ teaspoon salt
¾ teaspoon ground ginger
1 teaspoon ground cinnamon
½ teaspoon ground cloves
1 teaspoon pure vanilla extract
1¼ cups/2½ sticks butter, softened
1 cup dark brown sugar, firmly packed
1 egg
¼ cup molasses

1. Preheat the oven to 350°F. Grease two baking sheets.

2. In a large bowl and using an electric mixer, combine the flour, baking soda, salt, ginger, cinnamon, and cloves. Gradually add the vanilla, butter, sugar, egg, and molasses, increasing the speed to medium. Beat for 2 minutes, scraping down the sides of the bowl as necessary.

3. Drop large tablespoonfuls of the dough well apart onto the baking sheets. Bake until the tops are dry, 12–15 minutes. Let cool completely on wire racks.

COOKIE TIP
To prevent molasses from clinging to the side of the measuring cup, lightly grease the cup first or spray it with nonstick cooking spray.

OATMEAL RAISIN
Cookies

These classic American cookies have stood the test of time.
Be sure not to overcook them so that they stay nice and chewy.

MAKES: 10–12
BAKING TIME: 10 MINUTES

INGREDIENTS
Generous 1 cup all-purpose flour
1½ cups rolled oats
1 teaspoon ground ginger
½ teaspoon baking powder
½ teaspoon baking soda
¾ cup light brown sugar, lightly
   packed
⅓ cup raisins
1 egg, lightly beaten
½ cup vegetable oil
4 tablespoons milk

1. Preheat the oven to 400°F. Lightly grease a baking sheet. Mix together the flour, oats, ginger, baking powder, baking soda, sugar, and raisins in a large bowl.

2. In another bowl, mix together the egg, oil, and milk. Make a well in the center of the dry ingredients and pour in the egg mixture. Mix together well to make a soft dough.

3. Place spoonfuls of the dough well apart onto the baking sheet and flatten slightly with the tines of a fork. Bake until golden, about 10 minutes. Transfer the cookies to a wire rack to cool completely.

APPLE & CRANBERRY
Shortcake

These delicious fruity wedges of shortcake are great served as a dessert accompanied by a spoonful of sour cream.

1. Lightly grease a 9-inch round removable-bottomed pan.

2. To make the filling, peel, core, and slice the apples. Cook gently with 1 tablespoon water for about 5 minutes until the fruit is soft. Stir in the cranberry sauce and allow to cool.

3. Beat the butter and sugar together until light and fluffy. Beat in the egg and vanilla extract. Sift the flour and cornstarch together and beat in to form a soft dough.

4. Divide the dough in half and roll out one piece to fit the base of the prepared pan. Prick all over with a fork. Spread the fruit mixture over the dough, leaving a small border around the edge. Dampen the edges with a little water. Roll out the remaining dough and lightly press over the top. Chill for 30 minutes in the refrigerator or 10 minutes in the freezer.

5. Preheat the oven to 350°F. Bake in the center of the oven for 35–40 minutes until golden. Allow to cool in the pan. When cold, carefully remove from the pan and cut into wedges. Store in a cool place for up to three days.

MAKES: 12
BAKING TIME: 35–40 MINUTES

INGREDIENTS
$^3/_4$ cup/1$^1/_2$ sticks butter, softened
$^1/_3$ cup sugar
1 egg
1 teaspoon vanilla extract
2 cups self-rising flour
$^1/_2$ cup cornstarch
FILLING
2 green dessert apples
$^1/_3$ cup cranberry sauce

BLUEBERRY
THUMBPRINT Cookies

The simple, mellow vanilla flavor of these cookies works incredibly well with the tartness of the blueberry jelly. For a really traditional American taste, try filling the thumbprint well with peanut butter and jelly.

MAKES: 36
BAKING TIME: 10 MINUTES

INGREDIENTS
1 cup/2 sticks butter, softened
Scant 1 cup confectioners' sugar
1 teaspoon vanilla extract
Scant 1 cup ground almonds
Scant 1⅓ cups all-purpose flour
Blueberry jelly
Confectioners' sugar for dusting

1. Lightly grease two baking sheets. Cream the butter and sugar together until pale and fluffy, then beat in the vanilla. Blend in the ground almonds and then gradually add the flour, bringing the mixture together with your hands to form a soft dough as you add the last of the flour.

2. Lightly dust your hands with flour and roll the dough into small balls about the size of a walnut. Arrange on the baking sheets and using your thumb, make a deep hole in the center of each cookie. Chill for 30 minutes.

3. Preheat the oven to 350°F. Bake the cookies for 10 minutes, then fill each hole with a little jelly and return to the oven until pale golden, about 5 minutes. Let cool on the baking sheets for a few minutes before transferring to a wire rack to cool completely. Dust with confectioners' sugar to finish.

OATY APPLE
Crunchies

A special favorite with kids and adults, the crunchiness of the oats and moistness of the applesauce gives these cookies great appeal.

MAKES: 18
BAKING TIME: 10–15 MINUTES

INGREDIENTS

1¾ cups rolled oats
Generous ⅓ cup all-purpose flour
¾ cup light brown sugar, firmly
    packed
Scant ½ cup chunky applesauce
½ cup corn oil
1 egg

1. Preheat the oven to 350°F. Lightly grease two baking sheets.

2. Place all the ingredients in a large mixing bowl and beat until well combined.

3. Drop rounded tablespoons of the dough onto the baking sheets. Flatten slightly with the back of a spoon.

4. Bake until golden, 10–15 minutes. Let cool on the baking sheets for a few minutes then transfer to a wire rack to cool completely.

COOKIE TIP
If you are cooking with children make sure you clear a large area to work in—a small confined area may cause unnecessary accidents to happen.

MELTING Moments

These pretty cookies take their name from their fabulous melt-in-the-mouth dough.

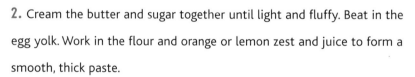

MAKES: 20
BAKING TIME: 15–20 MINUTES

INGREDIENTS
3/4 cup/1 1/2 sticks butter, softened
Scant 1/4 cup sugar
1 egg yolk
1 1/4 cups all-purpose flour
Grated zest of 1/2 orange or lemon
1 tablespoon orange or lemon juice
Mixed candied peel for decoration
Confectioners' sugar for dusting

1. Preheat the oven to 375°F.
Lightly grease two baking sheets.

2. Cream the butter and sugar together until light and fluffy. Beat in the egg yolk. Work in the flour and orange or lemon zest and juice to form a smooth, thick paste.

3. Spoon the paste into a pastry bag fitted with a large star tip and pipe rosettes measuring about 2 inches across onto the baking sheets. Lightly press some mixed candied peel into each cookie.

4. Bake until pale golden, 15–20 minutes. Let cool on the baking sheets for a few minutes before transferring to a wire rack to cool completely. Dust each cookie with confectioners' sugar.

COOKIE TIP
Only store one kind of cookie in a container. If you mix crisp and soft cookies they will all go soft and end up tasting the same.

STRAWBERRY JELLY Delights

Children will love helping to stamp out the circles and rings in these attractive cookies.

MAKES: 12–16
BAKING TIME: 15 MINUTES

INGREDIENTS
$\frac{1}{2}$ cup/1 stick butter, softened
$\frac{1}{4}$ cup sugar
1 egg
$\frac{1}{2}$ teaspoon vanilla extract
Scant $1\frac{1}{3}$ cups all-purpose flour
6 tablespoons cornstarch
$\frac{1}{2}$ teaspoon baking powder
FILLING
Strawberry or raspberry jelly

1. Cream the butter and sugar together until light and fluffy. Beat in the egg and vanilla. Sift the flour, cornstarch, and baking powder together and beat in to form a soft dough.

2. Preheat the oven to 350°F. Lightly grease two baking sheets.

3. Roll out the dough on a lightly floured counter to about $\frac{1}{8}$ inch thick and cut into circles using a $2\frac{1}{2}$-inch cookie cutter. Cut a 1-inch circle from the center of half the circles. The trimmings can be rerolled and used to make additional cookies. Make sure you have an equal number of circles and rings. Arrange on the baking sheets.

4. Bake until pale golden, about 15 minutes. Let cool on the baking sheets for a few minutes before transferring to a wire rack to cool completely.

5. When cooled completely, spread the circles with the jelly and place a ring on top, pushing lightly together. Store in an airtight container for up to one week.

SPICY CRANBERRY
Cookies

Dried cranberries can be bought sweetened or unsweetened. Sweetened berries resemble red raisins; unsweetened cranberries taste slightly tart.

MAKES: 15
BAKING TIME: 15–18 MINUTES

INGREDIENTS
½ cup/1 stick butter, softened
Scant ½ cup sugar
1 egg, separated
⅓ cup dried cranberries
1¼ cups all-purpose flour
½ teaspoon pumpkin pie spice
Demerara sugar for sprinkling

1. Preheat the oven to 350°F. Lightly grease two baking sheets. Cream the butter and sugar together until light and fluffy, then beat in the egg yolk. Stir in the cranberries.

2. Sift together the flour and spice. Add to the bowl and mix to form a stiff dough. Roll out the dough on a lightly floured counter to about ⅛ inch thick and cut into 3-inch circles.

3. Arrange on the baking sheets. Lightly beat the egg white and brush over the surface of each circle. Sprinkle with the Demerara sugar.

4. Bake until golden and brown, 15–18 minutes. Let cool for a few minutes on the baking sheets, then transfer to a wire rack to cool completely. Store in an airtight container for up to one week.

COOKIE TIP
If you have difficulty separating egg yolks from whites, tap the shell sharply and break the egg onto a saucer. Place an eggcup upside down over the yolk and tip the saucer so the white slides into the bowl.

OAT CRUNCH
Cookies

While the cookies are hot, press an indentation into the center of each one with your thumb and fill with a little jelly.

MAKES: 20
BAKING TIME: 16–18 MINUTES

INGREDIENTS
Scant 1 cup all-purpose flour
1 teaspoon baking soda
1¾ cups rolled oats
½ cup/1 stick butter
½ cup light brown sugar, firmly
  packed
1 tablespoon light corn syrup
1 tablespoon water

1. Preheat the oven to 350°F. Lightly grease two baking sheets. Sift the flour and baking soda into a mixing bowl. Stir in the oats.

2. Place the butter, sugar, corn syrup, and 1 tablespoon water in a pan and heat gently, stirring until combined. Add to the dry ingredients and stir until well mixed.

3. Take small amounts of the dough, each about the size of a walnut, and roll into balls. Space them well apart on the baking sheets and flatten slightly.

4. Bake until golden, 16–18 minutes. Let cool on the baking sheets for 2–3 minutes, then transfer to a wire rack to cool completely. Store in an airtight container for up to five days.

COOKIE TIP
Cool cookies on wire racks without touching each other to keep them from sticking together.

ALMOND Macaroons

Macaroons are traditionally made on edible rice paper, but if you have trouble finding it, then dust the baking sheets liberally with semolina and flour.

MAKES: **12**
BAKING TIME: **15–20 MINUTES**

INGREDIENTS
$2/3$ cup ground almonds
$3/4$ cup superfine sugar
2 tablespoons semolina or ground
    rice
2 egg whites
Few drops of almond extract
$1/2$ cup semisweet chocolate chips
Whole blanched almonds for
    decoration

1. Preheat the oven to 325°F. Line two baking sheets with rice paper.

2. Mix the almonds, sugar, and semolina. In a separate bowl, beat the egg whites until stiff. Add the almond extract.

3. Gradually fold in the sugar and almond mixture until quite stiff.

4. Fold in the chocolate chips. Place tablespoonful of mixture onto the baking sheets, well spaced out. Place an almond on top of each and bake until golden, 15–20 minutes. Cool, then tear the rice paper between each biscuit, or use a wire rack if you're not using paper.

COOKIE TIP
Baked and uncooked shaped cookies can be frozen for up to two months. Thaw baked cookies at room temperature and bake uncooked ones from frozen.

HONEY
Cookies

Orange and walnut flavored cookies dipped in honey for a real old-fashioned taste.

MAKES: 30
BAKING TIME: 15–20 MINUTES

INGREDIENTS
$^1/_2$ cup/1 stick butter
Finely grated zest of 1 orange
$^1/_3$ cup superfine sugar
$^1/_3$ cup sunflower oil
2 cups all-purpose flour
1 cup self-rising flour
$^1/_4$ cup finely chopped walnuts
$^2/_3$ cup orange juice
1 cup honey
2 tablespoons finely chopped walnuts for sprinkling

1. Preheat the oven to 350°F. Put the butter, orange zest, and sugar into a bowl and beat well together. Gradually beat in the oil until the mixture is light and fluffy.

2. Stir in the flours, nuts, and juice and mix to a soft dough.

3. Using two tablespoons shape the mixture into ovals and place on baking sheets lined with parchment paper. Bake in the oven for 15–20 minutes until lightly browned.

4. Heat the honey in a small saucepan. Making sure the honey is not too hot, dip the warm biscuits in the honey to coat. Place on a wire rack over a tray. Sprinkle with the chopped nuts.

COOKIE TIP
Make sure the honey glaze has set completely before transferring the cookies to a storage container.

DUTCH
Shortcakes

Crisp buttery shortcakes baked in strips and then cut up.

MAKES: 18
BAKING TIME: 15–20 MINUTES

INGREDIENTS

2 tablespoons custard powder (or cornstarch)
1½ cups all-purpose flour
⅔ cup butter
⅓ cup superfine sugar
1 egg yolk

1. Preheat the oven to 350°F. Sift the custard powder and flour together.

2. Cream the butter and sugar together and beat in the egg yolk. Mix in the flour well.

3. Put the mixture into a pastry bag fitted with a large star tip and pipe three flat zigzag lines about 2 x 10 inches on a nonstick baking sheet.

4. Bake in the oven for 15–20 minutes until pale golden brown. While still warm cut each piece into six and cool on a wire rack.

COOKIE TIP

If you are looking out for your health you may be considering replacing the butter with low fat margarine, but be aware that reducing the sugar and fat in the ingredients can make cookies more cake-like.

FIG & DATE Rolls

Short crumbly pastry filled with moist dates and figs. These cookies keep well in an airtight container.

MAKES: 24
BAKING TIME: 20–25 MINUTES

INGREDIENTS

FILLING
1³/₄ cups dried figs, finely chopped
¹/₂ cup stoned dates, finely chopped
¹/₂ cup water
Finely grated zest of 1 lemon
¹/₂ cup superfine sugar

DOUGH
¹/₂ cup/1 stick butter
¹/₃ cup superfine sugar
1 teaspoon ground cinnamon
1 egg
¹/₂ cup ground almonds
2 cups all-purpose flour

1. To make the filling put all the ingredients into a pan and stir over a gentle heat until the sugar is dissolved. Simmer uncovered for about 15 minutes until the mixture is thick and pulpy. Cool.

2. To make the dough beat together the butter, sugar, cinnamon, and egg. Stir in the ground almonds and flour. Knead lightly and divide into four. Wrap each portion in plastic wrap and chill for 30 minutes.

3. Preheat the oven to 350°F. Roll out each portion of dough between sheets of parchment paper to 4 x 8 inches. Spread a quarter of the filling along each rectangle leaving a ¹/₂-inch border. Fold the long sides over the filling to meet in the center and press gently together. Tuck the ends under.

4. Place the rolls seam side down, on nonstick baking sheets. Bake for 20–25 minutes until lightly browned. Remove and let cool.

5. When cold cut into slices.

CARDAMOM GINGER Crisps

Ideal for dunking these crisp little fingers have the unusual addition of ground cardamom.

MAKES: 50
BAKING TIME: 10–15 MINUTES

INGREDIENTS

½ cup/1 stick butter
⅔ cup light brown sugar
1 teaspoon ground cardamom
½ teaspoon ground cinnamon
Pinch of ground nutmeg
2 egg yolks
1½ cups all-purpose flour
2 tablespoons candied ginger, finely chopped

1. Put the butter, sugar, spices, and egg yolks into a bowl and beat well together.

2. Stir in the flour and candied ginger. Knead until smooth. Shape into a block about 3 x 11 inches. Wrap in parchment paper and chill until firm.

3. Preheat the oven to 325°F. Cut the dough into ⅛-inch slices and place on baking sheets lined with parchment paper. Bake in the oven for 10–15 minutes until golden. Cool on a wire rack.

COOKIE TIP
Always stir flour prior to measuring. Flour settles as it sits and if you do not stir it you may end up adding too much to your cookies.

APPLE STREUSEL
Bars

These fruity, crunchy bars make a wonderful afternoon snack with a cup of tea.

MAKES: 12–14
BAKING TIME: 45 MINUTES

INGREDIENTS

2 cups self-rising flour
¼ cup ground almonds
¾ cup/1½ sticks butter
⅓ cup light brown sugar
2 egg yolks

TOPPING

3 dessert apples
½ cup golden raisins (optional)
1½ cups all-purpose flour
½ teaspoon ground cloves
¾ stick butter
⅓ cup brown sugar

1. Preheat the oven to 350°F. Lightly grease an 8 x 11-inch oblong baking pan.

2. Sift the self-rising flour into a mixing bowl and stir in the almonds. Cut the butter into cubes and blend into the mixture until it resembles bread crumbs. Stir in the brown sugar. Add the egg yolks and work the mixture together to form a firm dough. Press out to line the base of the prepared pan. Prick all over and chill while making the topping.

3. To make the topping, peel, core, and roughly chop the apples, then place in a pan with 2 tablespoons water. Cook gently for about 3–4 minutes until tender. Stir in the golden raisins if using.

4. Sift the flour and cloves into another bowl. Blend in the butter until the mixture resembles crumbs. Stir in the brown sugar. Spread the apple mixture over the dough and sprinkle the streusel mixture on top. Bake for about 45 minutes until the topping is golden.

5. Cool in the pan and serve cut into bars or squares. Store in the refrigerator for up to four days.

LAVENDER SCENTED
Shortbread

A popular remedy in traditional medicine, lavender is said to help promote sleep. Try one of these fragrant shortbreads before going to bed and they should really do the trick.

MAKES: 18–20
BAKING TIME: 15–20 MINUTES

INGREDIENTS

¹⁄₂ cup superfine sugar
4 dried lavender flowers, natural and
    unsprayed
1 cup butter
2 cups all-purpose white flour
1 cup ground rice
Pinch of salt
Extra lavender flowers and superfine
    sugar for decoration

1. Line two baking sheets with waxed paper.

2. Put the sugar and lavender in a food processor and whiz for about 10 seconds.

3. Cream together the butter and sugar until light and fluffy, then stir in the flour, ground rice, and salt until the mixture resembles bread crumbs.

4. Using your hands, gather the dough together and knead until it forms a ball. Roll into a sausage shape and then shape into a long block about 2 inches thick. Wrap in plastic wrap and chill for about 30 minutes, or until firm.

5. Preheat the oven to 375°F. Slice the dough into ¹⁄₄-inch squares and place on the baking sheets. Bake for 15–20 minutes, or until pale golden. Sprinkle with sugar and leave on the baking sheets for 10 minutes, then transfer to a wire rack to cool completely.

GOURMET
COOKIES

WHITE CHOCOLATE & NUT Cookies

If you prefer, substitute the macadamias for another variety of nut.

MAKES: 12–15
BAKING TIME: 15–18 MINUTES

INGREDIENTS
Generous 1¾ cups all-purpose flour
1 teaspoon baking soda
¼ cup unsweetened cocoa powder
½ teaspoon salt
1 cup/2 sticks unsalted butter, softened
1½ cups light brown sugar, firmly packed
Scant ½ cup sugar
2 large eggs
2 teaspoons vanilla extract
Scant 1⅓ cups white chocolate chips
2 cups macadamia nuts, coarsely chopped

1. Preheat the oven to 375°F. Lightly grease two baking sheets.

2. In a medium bowl, sift together the flour, baking soda, cocoa powder, and salt. Set aside.

3. Cream the butter and sugars together until light and fluffy. Beat in the eggs and vanilla. Gently stir in the flour mixture until just combined. Fold in the white chocolate and macadamia nuts.

4. Drop large rounded tablespoons of the dough onto the baking sheets, well spaced apart as the cookies will spread. Bake until firm, 15–18 minutes. Let cool on the baking sheets for a few minutes before transferring to a wire rack to cool completely.

COOKIE TIP
Pack even more of a chocolate punch by adding some semisweet chocolate chips.

ORANGE PECAN Cookies

These cookies will keep in an airtight container—
if you can resist eating them all at once.

MAKES: 24
BAKING TIME: 10–12 MINUTES

INGREDIENTS
6 tablespoons/¾ stick butter
6 tablespoons sugar
6 tablespoons light brown sugar,
   firmly packed
1 egg
Grated zest of 1 orange
2 tablespoons orange juice
1¼ cups all-purpose flour
½ teaspoon baking soda
¾ cup pecans, coarsely chopped

1. Preheat the oven to 350°F. Lightly grease two baking sheets.

2. Cream the butter and sugars together until pale and fluffy. Beat in the egg, orange zest, and juice.

3. Sift the flour and baking soda together and beat into the mixture. Stir in the nuts.

4. Drop tablespoons of the dough well apart onto the baking sheets. Bake until golden, 10–12 minutes. Let the cookies cool on the baking sheets for 2–3 minutes, then transfer to a wire rack to cool completely. Store in an airtight container for up to five days.

COOKIE TIP
Add a few of the chopped nuts to the top of the cookies before baking to give an extra crunch.

PINEAPPLE

Macaroons

Enjoy these soft, fruity macaroons with midmorning coffee or afternoon tea.

MAKES: 20–24
BAKING TIME: 25–30 MINUTES

INGREDIENTS

14 ounces canned pineapple rings in natural juice
10–12 candied cherries
3 egg whites
Scant 1 cup sugar
Generous 2½ cups flaked coconut

COOKIE TIP

Vary the flavoring in these chewy cookies or leave out the pineapple if you prefer a traditional macaroon.

1. Preheat the oven to 325°F. Line two baking sheets with nonstick parchment paper.

2. Drain the pineapple well and chop finely. Place in a strainer and squeeze out as much juice as possible. Halve the cherries.

3. Beat the egg whites to stiff peaks. Gradually beat in the sugar. Fold in the pineapple and coconut until well combined.

4. Drop spoonfuls of the dough onto the lined baking sheets, piling into a pyramid shape. Allow space for the cookies to spread slightly. Top each with half a cherry.

5. Bake until lightly browned and crisp, 25–30 minutes. Let cool on the baking sheets, then carefully remove and store in an airtight container for up to three days. Do not freeze.

SPICED PUMPKIN & PECAN Crisps

These slightly spiced cookies are a great light snack.

MAKES: 24–30
BAKING TIME: 25–30 MINUTES

INGREDIENTS

¹/₂ cup/1 stick butter, softened
Scant 1 cup all-purpose flour
³/₄ cup light brown sugar, lightly
   packed
²/₃ cup canned pumpkin or cooked
   and mashed pumpkin
1 egg
2 teaspoons ground cinnamon
¹/₂ teaspoon vanilla extract
¹/₂ teaspoon baking powder
1 teaspoon baking soda
¹/₂ teaspoon ground nutmeg
Scant ¹/₂ cup whole-wheat flour
²/₃ cup pecans, roughly chopped
1 cup raisins

FROSTING

¹/₂ cup/¹/₂ stick unsalted butter
1¹/₂ cups confectioners' sugar
1¹/₂ teaspoons vanilla extract
2 tablespoons milk

1. Preheat the oven to 375°F. Lightly grease two baking sheets.

2. Using an electric beater, beat the butter until fluffy. Add the flour, sugar, pumpkin, egg, cinnamon, vanilla, baking powder, baking soda, and nutmeg. Beat until well combined, scraping down the sides of the bowl. Add the whole-wheat flour, nuts, and raisins and fold in until just combined.

3. Drop the dough in large tablespoonfuls, well spaced apart onto the baking sheets. Bake until golden, 25–30 minutes. Remove from the oven and let cool on a wire rack.

4. To make the frosting, melt the butter over a medium heat in a small pan and continue cooking until light golden brown. Remove from the heat and add the confectioners' sugar, vanilla, and milk. Mix until smooth, adding a little more milk or confectioners' sugar as necessary to make the mixture spreadable. Let cool until thick, then spread generously over the cooled cookies.

DARK CHOCOLATE & PECAN Brownies

Have a batch of these rich, sticky brownies ready for a midnight treat—served with a big scoop of ice cream.

MAKES: 12
BAKING TIME: 20–25 MINUTES

INGREDIENTS
4 ounces bittersweet chocolate
¾ cup/1½ sticks butter
2 cups granulated sugar
3 eggs
1¾ cups all-purpose flour
1½ teaspoons vanilla extract
1 cup pecan nuts

1. Preheat the oven to 350°F. Butter a 13 x 9-inch nonstick baking pan. Break the bittersweet chocolate into pieces and place in a pan with the butter. Melt over a gentle heat, stirring occasionally, and then take the pan off the heat.

2. Add the sugar to the chocolate and stir until dissolved. Beat in the eggs, and then stir in the flour, vanilla extract, and pecan nuts. Pour the mixture into the pan and level the surface.

3. Bake for 20–25 minutes, or until the top of the brownies are shiny and set. Place the pan of brownies on a wire rack to cool, then cut into squares and serve.

COOKIE TIP
If you can keep your hands off them for long enough, these cookies will keep for several days in an airtight container.

WALNUT

Kisses

When grinding walnuts for these cookies, use on and off pulses of the food processor to prevent them from turning to paste.

MAKES: 40
BAKING TIME: 30 MINUTES

INGREDIENTS
Scant ½ cup walnuts
Scant 1 cup confectioners' sugar
2 egg whites

COOKIE TIP
*Almonds
work just as well
as walnuts in this
recipe.*

1. Preheat the oven to 300°F. Line two baking sheets with nonstick parchment paper.

2. Grind the walnuts in a food processor until very finely chopped. Sift the confectioners' sugar into a bowl.

3. Put the egg white in a large, greasefree mixing bowl and beat until frothy. Gradually add the confectioners' sugar and beat until combined.

4. Place the bowl over a pan of gently simmering water and beat until the mixture is very thick and stands in stiff peaks. Remove from the pan and beat until cold.

5. Carefully fold in the ground walnuts until just blended, then spoon into a pastry bag fitted with a large plain or star tip. Pipe small rosettes or balls slightly spaced onto the baking sheets.

6. Bake until the cookies can be easily removed from the paper, about 30 minutes. Let cool and store in an airtight container.

FROSTED COFFEE

Creams

Simple to make with a sophisticated flavor, these frosted cookies are delicious with morning coffee.

MAKES: **20**
BAKING TIME: **15 MINUTES**

INGREDIENTS
½ cup/1 stick butter, softened
Scant ½ cup sugar
¼ cup strong black coffee
Generous 1⅔ cups all-purpose flour
3 tablespoons cornstarch

FILLING
¼ cup/½ stick butter, softened
1⅓ cups confectioners' sugar
2 tablespoons strong black coffee

FROSTING
⅔ cup confectioners' sugar
1–2 teaspoons strong black coffee

1. Preheat the oven to 350°F. Lightly grease two baking sheets.

2. Cream the butter and sugar together until light and fluffy. Beat in the remaining ingredients, bringing the mixture together to form a firm dough.

3. Roll out the dough on a lightly floured counter to about ⅛ inch thick and cut out with cookie cutter shapes of your choice. Arrange on baking sheets.

4. Bake until lightly browned, about 15 minutes. Let cool on the baking sheets for a few minutes before transferring to a wire rack to cool completely.

5. To make the filling, cream the butter until fluffy, then gradually beat in the confectioners' sugar and coffee. Sandwich the cookies together in pairs with the filling.

6. To make the frosting, sift the confectioners' sugar into a bowl and stir in enough coffee to form a smooth frosting. Spread over the tops of the cookies and let set.

LACE
Cookies

You can make these cookies slightly larger than usual as they look lovely piled up and served with ice cream or elegant cream desserts.

MAKES: 12–14
BAKING TIME: 5–7 MINUTES

INGREDIENTS
⅓ cup butter
¾ cup rolled oats
½ cup superfine sugar
1 egg, beaten
2 teaspoons all-purpose flour
1 teaspoon baking soda
½ teaspoon ground cinnamon

1. Preheat the oven to 350°F. Line baking sheets with parchment paper. Melt the butter in a pan and remove from the heat. Stir in all the remaining ingredients.

2. Put 3–4 heaping teaspoonfuls of the mixture onto the prepared baking sheets.

3. Bake in the oven for about 5–7 minutes or until dark golden brown.

4. Leave to cool for a few minutes on the baking sheets and then carefully remove to a wire rack using a large spatula.

COOKIE TIP
Don't be tempted to put more than three or four of these cookies on the baking sheet and make sure they are spaced well apart.

PISTACHIO Biscotti

Decorate these cookies by drizzling a little chocolate over the top.

MAKES: 50
BAKING TIME: 40 MINUTES

INGREDIENTS
Generous 1⅓ cups pistachios
Generous 3 cups all-purpose flour
Generous ⅔ cup coarse cornmeal
2 teaspoons baking powder
½ cup/1 stick butter
Scant ½ cup sugar
3 eggs
1 teaspoon grated lemon zest
1 teaspoon grated orange zest
2 tablespoons orange juice
½ teaspoon almond extract
1 teaspoon fennel seeds, crushed
  (optional)

1. Preheat the oven to 350°F. Lightly grease two baking sheets.

2. Coarsely chop half the pistachios. Sift the flour, cornmeal, and baking powder together.

3. Cream the butter and sugar together until pale and fluffy. Beat in the eggs one at a time. Beat in the lemon and orange zest, juice, almond extract, and fennel seeds. Do not worry if the mixture looks curdled at this stage, as this is normal.

4. Beat in the chopped and whole pistachios. Finally, work in the flour mixture, using your hands to mix it to a soft dough. Divide the dough into four pieces and roll each piece into a log shape about 12 inches long on a lightly floured counter. Place on the baking sheets and flatten slightly.

5. Bake until the logs are risen and golden, about 30 minutes; reverse the baking sheets half way through the baking time. Remove from the oven and let cool slightly.

6. Reduce the oven temperature to 325°F. When the logs are cool enough to handle, cut each one diagonally into ½-inch slices. Arrange cut-side down on the baking sheets and return to the oven until crisp and golden, about 10 minutes. Store in an airtight container for up to two weeks.

LIME BROWN SUGAR Cookies

The lime frosting lends a real tang to these sophisticated cookies.

MAKES: **22**
BAKING TIME: **10–12 MINUTES**

INGREDIENTS
½ cup/1 stick butter
½ cup light brown sugar, firmly
  packed
1 egg, beaten
Grated peel of 1 lime
1 tablespoon lime juice
Generous 2 cups all-purpose flour
1 teaspoon baking soda

FROSTING
Generous 1¼ cups confectioners'
  sugar
1–2 tablespoons fresh lime juice
Grated zest of 1 lime

1. Preheat the oven to 350°F. Lightly grease two baking sheets. Cream the butter and brown sugar together until fluffy. Beat in the egg, lime zest, and juice.

2. Sift together the flour and baking soda, then beat into the butter mixture. Work together with your hands to form a soft dough.

3. On a lightly floured counter, roll out the dough to ¼ inch thick and cut out cookies with cookie cutters. Place on the baking sheets and bake until crisp and golden, 10–12 minutes. Let cool on the baking sheets for 2–3 minutes, then transfer to a wire rack to cool completely.

4. To make the frosting, sift the confectioners' sugar into a bowl and mix in the lime juice and zest until smooth. Spread or pipe over the cookies. Let dry for 1–2 hours or until the frosting has set. Store in an airtight container for up to five days.

CHEESECAKE SWIRL Brownies

These are irresistible—a chocolate brownie base topped with brownie mixture and cream cheese. Cut into small squares to serve as they are rather rich but perfectly heavenly and make a great dessert when served with fresh raspberries.

MAKES: **16**
BAKING TIME: **30 MINUTES**

INGREDIENTS

CHEESECAKE MIX

1 egg
1 cup full-fat cream cheese
¼ cup superfine sugar
1 teaspoon vanilla extract

BROWNIE MIX

4 ounces bittersweet chocolate
½ cup/1 stick unsalted butter
¾ cup light brown sugar
2 eggs, beaten
½ cup all-purpose flour

1. Preheat the oven to 325°F. Grease and base line an 8-inch square shallow cake pan.

2. To make the cheesecake mixture put all the ingredients into a bowl and beat well together.

3. To make the brownie mixture: melt the chocolate and butter together in a bowl in the microwave or over a pan of hot water. When melted, remove from the heat, stir well and stir in the sugar. Add the eggs a little at a time and beat well. Gently fold in the flour.

4. Spread two-thirds of the brownie mixture in the base of the prepared pan. Spread the cheesecake mixture on top. Spoon the remaining brownie mixture on top in heaps. Using a skewer, swirl the mixtures together.

5. Bake in the oven for about 30 minutes or until just set in the center. Leave to cool in the pan and then cut into squares.

FLORENTINES

Sweet and rich these are great with after-dinner coffee and liqueurs.

MAKES: **12**
BAKING TIME: **7–10 MINUTES**

INGREDIENTS

¼ cup/1½ sticks unsalted butter

¼ cup superfine sugar

2 tablespoons heavy cream

2 tablespoons chopped candied angelica

3 tablespoons chopped mixed candied peel

3 tablespoons golden raisins

5 candied cherries, chopped

⅓ cup flaked almonds, lightly crushed

1 tablespoon all-purpose flour

4 ounces bittersweet or white chocolate, chopped

1. Preheat the oven to 350°F. Put the butter and sugar into a small pan and heat gently until dissolved then bring to a boil.

2. Remove from the heat and stir in all the ingredients except the chocolate. Mix well together.

3. Place heaping teaspoonfuls on lightly greased or nonstick baking sheets. Space well apart to allow for spreading. Bake a few at time for about 6–8 minutes until the edges are just beginning to turn brown. Using a large plain metal cookie cutter push the edges of each Florentine in to create a neat round. Bake for 1–2 minutes more until golden brown.

4. Allow to cool on the baking sheet for a few minutes then transfer to a wire rack to harden.

5. Melt the chocolate in a heatproof bowl over a pan of simmering water. Roll the edges of each cookie in the chocolate and place on a sheet of parchment paper until set.

COOKIE TIP
Rolling half the cookies in bittersweet chocolate and the other half in white makes them into a real treat.

BRAZIL NUT

Biscotti

Italians traditionally dunk their biscotti—a cookie native to their country—into espresso or vin santo (sweet wine).

MAKES: **50**
BAKING TIME: **50 MINUTES**

INGREDIENTS

2 eggs
Generous ¾ cup sugar
Grated zest 1 orange
2 tablespoons orange juice
¼ cup light vegetable oil
1⅓ cups Brazil nuts
2⅓ cups all-purpose flour
2 teaspoons baking powder
Scant 1 cup ground rice

1. Preheat the oven to 350°F.

2. Place the eggs and sugar in a large mixing bowl and beat until very pale and thick. Beat in the orange zest, juice, and oil. Stir in the nuts.

3. Sift the flour and baking powder together and add to the bowl with the rice, working the mixture with your hands to form a soft dough. Add a little extra flour if the dough is too sticky. Divide in half and roll each piece to form an 8-inch log.

4. Place the logs on the baking sheets and bake until risen and golden, about 30 minutes. Remove from the oven and let cool slightly. Reduce the oven temperature to 300°F.

5. Using a serrated knife, cut the logs into thin slices and arrange on the baking sheets. Bake the slices, turning once, until crisp and golden on both sides, about 20 minutes. Store in an airtight container for several weeks.

MAPLE SYRUP
Tuiles

These little treats are a great accompaniment to creamy desserts. They do require a little care when cooking. Only cook two or three at a time, as they need to be shaped fairly quickly while still very warm.

MAKES: 20
BAKING TIME: 5–7 MINUTES

INGREDIENTS

¼ cup/½ stick unsalted butter
⅓ cup light brown sugar
1 tablespoon maple syrup
1 tablespoon brandy
⅓ cup all-purpose flour

COOKIE TIP
These tuiles can soften if left out, so store in an airtight container.

1. Preheat the oven to 350°F. Put the butter, sugar, and syrup into a pan and heat gently while stirring until the sugar has dissolved. Simmer, uncovered and without stirring, for 2 minutes.

2. Remove from the heat and stir in the brandy and flour. Put 2 or 3 level teaspoonfuls onto lightly greased baking sheets. Bake in the oven for 5–7 minutes until lightly browned.

3. Remove from the oven and cool for just 1 minute and then carefully lift off the baking sheet with a spatula. Drape over a wooden rolling pin or wooden spoon handle and leave to harden. Alternatively, pinch the center together to give a flower shape or drape over upturned eggcups to make little baskets.

CRACKLE
Cookies

These look stunning and are so easy to make. As a variation try adding some chopped dark candied cherries to the mixture.

MAKES: 24
BAKING TIME: 10 MINUTES

INGREDIENTS
½ cup self-rising flour
¼ cup unsweetened cocoa powder
½ cup superfine sugar
2 tablespoons/¼ stick butter
1 egg, beaten
1 teaspoon cherry brandy
½ cup confectioners' sugar

1. Preheat the oven to 400°F. Sift the flour and cocoa into a bowl and stir in the sugar.

2. Blend in the butter until the mixture resembles fine crumbs. Stir in the egg and cherry brandy and mix well together.

3. Put the confectioners' sugar into a bowl. Shape walnut-sized pieces of dough into balls and drop into the confectioners' sugar. Toss until thickly coated and place on baking sheets lined with parchment paper.

4. Bake for about 10 minutes until just set. Cool on a wire rack.

COOKIE TIP
If you wish you can make the dough ahead of time and keep covered in the refrigerator. Shape and bake the cookies at the last minute and serve warm.

POPPYSEED & HONEY Pinwheels

You can change the nuts and flavorings in these cookies. Try using chopped toasted almonds or macadamias, and for flavor try lemon instead of orange zest or a large pinch of ground cinnamon or ginger.

MAKES: 30
BAKING TIME: 8–10 MINUTES

INGREDIENTS
½ cup/1 stick butter
½ teaspoon vanilla extract
½ cup superfine sugar
1 egg
1⅔ cups all-purpose flour
FILLING
⅓ cup very finely chopped toasted
   hazelnuts
½ cup poppyseeds
¼ cup honey, warmed
1 teaspoon finely grated orange zest

1. Put the butter, vanilla, sugar, and egg into a bowl and beat well together. Stir in the flour and shape into a ball. Wrap in plastic wrap and chill until firm.

2. Put all the filling ingredients into a bowl and mix well together. Cut the dough in half and roll out each portion between sheets of parchment paper, to a rectangle 8 x 10 inches. Spread the filling over the two pieces of dough and roll up from the short side like a jelly roll. Wrap in plastic wrap and chill until firm.

3. Preheat the oven to 375°F. Cut the rolls into ⅛-inch slices and place on nonstick baking sheets. Bake for about 8–10 minutes until lightly browned.

COOKIE TIP
The pastry dough is very soft to handle so make sure it is well chilled before rolling out between sheets of parchment paper.

COOKIES
PLUS

CAPPUCCINO
Bars

The sheer variety of textures in these bars makes for a decadent treat.

MAKES: 12

INGREDIENTS

⅓ cup golden raisins
½ cup hot strong black coffee
10 ounces graham crackers
½ cup mini-marshmallows
8 ounces semisweet chocolate
¼ cup/½ stick butter

TOPPING

8 ounces white chocolate
¼ cup/½ stick butter
Scant 1 cup confectioners' sugar
Grated semisweet chocolate

1. Lightly grease an 8 x 8-inch square pan and line the bottom with nonstick parchment paper.

2. Soak the raisins in the hot coffee for 5 minutes. Break the graham crackers into small pieces and place in a bowl with the marshmallows. Sprinkle in the coffee and soaked raisins.

3. Melt the chocolate and butter in a microwave or in a bowl set over hot water. Add to the graham cracker mixture and stir until well coated. Press the mixture into the prepared cake pan and let chill until firm.

4. To make the topping, melt the white chocolate in a microwave or in a bowl set over a pan of hot water. Let cool. Cream the butter until soft, gradually beat in the confectioners' sugar. Beat in the melted white chocolate. Spread the mixture over the graham cracker base and let set.

5. Sprinkle with grated chocolate and cut into bars. Store in an airtight container in a cool place for up to four days.

APPLE & RASPBERRY Bars

Apples and raspberries are a wonderfully irresistible combination.

MAKES: 12–14
BAKING TIME: 45 MINUTES

INGREDIENTS

6 tablespoons/$^1/_3$ cup unsalted butter
$^3/_4$ cup superfine sugar
3 eggs
1 teaspoon vanilla extract
1$^1/_2$ cups self-rising flour
4 medium cooking apples (about
   1 pound), grated
6 ounces raspberries

1. Preheat the oven to 375°F. Grease a 15 x 10 x 1-inch baking pan and set aside.

2. In a large mixing bowl beat the butter with the sugar until it resembles fine bread crumbs. Beat in the eggs and vanilla extract until combined.

3. Beat or stir in the flour, and then add the grated apple. Mix thoroughly until well combined.

4. Pour the batter into the prepared baking pan, spreading the mixture evenly. Push the raspberries into the mixture evenly spaced around the tin. Bake for about 25 minutes or until a tester inserted in the center comes out clean.

5. Cool in the pan and serve cut into bars or squares. Store in the refrigerator for up to four days.

CHOCOLATE & MACADAMIA NUT Bars

These bars will set as they cool, but still be wonderfully chewy.

MAKES: 9
BAKING TIME: 30–35 MINUTES

INGREDIENTS

1 cup/2 sticks butter
8 ounces semisweet chocolate, cut up
¾ cup macadamia nuts
1¼ cups light brown sugar
3 eggs
2 cups all-purpose flour
2 teaspoons baking powder
½ teaspoon salt

1. Preheat the oven to 350°F. Melt the butter and chocolate together in a glass bowl over a pan of simmering water until smooth and glossy. Let it cool slightly. Toast the macadamia nuts on a baking sheet in the oven for 5 minutes until just golden, then roughly chop.

2. Beat the sugar and eggs together in a large bowl. Carefully stir in the chocolate mixture. Fold in the flour, baking powder, and salt, then stir in the chopped nuts.

3. Line the bottom of an 8-inch square, nonstick cake pan that is at least 2 inches deep. Pour in the mixture and bake for 30–35 minutes. Allow to cool in the pan.

4. Serve cut into squares with ice cream or cream.

MOCHA MUD Pies

A cookie that's rich and dense in texture like a brownie with a chocolate/coffee flavor has to be divine, and it is. Make sure the mixture is well chilled before baking.

MAKES: 16
BAKING TIME: 10 MINUTES

INGREDIENTS

¼ cup all-purpose flour

¼ teaspoon baking soda

7 ounces bittersweet chocolate, coarsely chopped

2 tablespoons/¼ stick unsalted butter

2–3 tablespoons instant coffee granules, according to personal taste

2 large eggs

½ cup superfine sugar

1 teaspoon vanilla extract

2 ounces semisweet chocolate chips

1. Sift together the flour and baking soda. Put the chocolate and the butter into a heatproof bowl over a pan of simmering water or melt in the microwave. When melted remove from the heat and stir in the coffee granules.

2. Put the eggs and sugar into a bowl and beat with an electric beater until pale and very thick. Stir in the chocolate mixture and the vanilla. Add the flour mixture and stir. Mix in the chocolate chips.

3. Cover the bowl and place in the refrigerator for about 1 hour.

4. Preheat the oven to 350°F. Line baking sheets with parchment paper. Place spoonfuls of the mixture well apart on the prepared sheets.

5. Bake for about 10 minutes or until the cookies feel just set when touched lightly with a finger. Cool for a few minutes before transferring to a wire rack.

BLONDIES

These are like brownies but are made with white chocolate and sugar instead of brown—even more irresistible.

MAKES: 18
BAKING TIME: 30–35 MINUTES

INGREDIENTS
1 pound 2 ounces white chocolate
$\frac{1}{3}$ cup butter
3 eggs
$\frac{3}{4}$ cup superfine sugar
$1\frac{1}{2}$ cups self-rising flour
2 cups macadamia nuts, roughly chopped
1 teaspoon vanilla extract

1. Preheat the oven to 375°F. Grease and base line a $10\frac{1}{2}$ x $7\frac{1}{2}$-inch baking pan.

2. Roughly chop 12 ounces of the chocolate and put aside.

3. Melt the remaining chocolate and the butter in a bowl over a pan of simmering water. Cool slightly.

4. Beat the eggs and sugar together in a bowl and gradually beat in the melted chocolate. Sift the flour over the mixture and fold in together with the chopped nuts, reserved chocolate, and vanilla extract.

5. Pour into the prepared pan and bake for 30–35 minutes until the center is only just firm to the touch. Cool in the pan. Cut into squares when cold.

COOKIE TIP
Store bar cookies either in tightly covered containers or in the pan in which they were baked. Make sure you cover the pan tightly with aluminum foil.

GRANOLA, HONEY & DATE Health Bars

Although granola is packed full of goodness, it can be very high in calories. Read the labels of packaged granola when buying to make sure that these bars have all the health benefits of granola without the fat!

MAKES: 10
BAKING TIME: 20–25 MINUTES

INGREDIENTS
Scant ¾ cup/1¼ sticks butter
6 tablespoons light brown sugar, firmly packed
¼ cup honey
Scant 1¼ cups granola
¾ cup rolled oats
⅔ cup dates, chopped

1. Preheat the oven to 375°F. Grease an 8 x 8-inch square cake pan and line the bottom with nonstick parchment paper.

2. Melt the butter with the sugar and honey in a pan, stirring thoroughly until well combined.

3. Remove from the heat and stir in the granola, oats, and dates. Turn into the cake pan and press down lightly. Bake until firm, 20–25 minutes.

4. Let cool for a few minutes in the pan, then cut into bars and let cool completely. Store in an airtight container for up to two weeks.

COOKIE TIP
For even cooking bake the bars on the middle shelf of your oven.

HAZELNUT & CHOCOLATE Bars

Toasting the hazelnuts in this recipe really brings out the nutty flavor.

MAKES: 12
BAKING TIME: 25 MINUTES

INGREDIENTS

3 ounces semisweet chocolate

½ cup/1 stick butter, softened

¼ cup light brown sugar, firmly packed

⅔ cup all-purpose flour

¾ cup rolled oats

12 tablespoons chocolate hazelnut spread, such as Nutella

⅓ cup hazelnuts, chopped and toasted

1. Preheat the oven to 350°F. Lightly grease an 8 x 8-inch square cake pan and line the bottom with nonstick parchment paper.

2. Melt the chocolate in a microwave or in a bowl set over a pan of simmering water. Cream the butter and sugar together until light and fluffy. Beat in the chocolate, then mix in the flour and oats to form a soft dough.

3. Press the mixture into the bottom of the prepared pan and bake until just golden, about 25 minutes.

4. Let cool in the pan. Remove from the pan and spread with chocolate hazelnut spread. Sprinkle with the hazelnuts and press lightly into the spread. Cut into bars. Store in a cool place, in a single layer in an airtight container, for up to one week.

COOKIE TIP

Keep the dough in the freezer for those chocolate cookie urges. Just remember to thaw the dough in the refrigerator for several hours for easier slicing.

NUTTY BUBBLE

Bars

A treat for all those peanut lovers and a great way to use up leftover cereal.

MAKES: 24

INGREDIENTS
½ cup/1 stick butter
⅓ cup light corn syrup
⅓ cup smooth peanut butter
½ cup superfine sugar
2 cups rice bubble cereal
2 cups coco bubble cereal
2 ounces peanut brittle, chopped
½ cup chopped toasted hazelnuts
White chocolate, melted, for drizzling

1. Base line a 9½ x 12-inch baking pan with parchment paper.

2. Mix together the butter, corn syrup, peanut butter, and sugar in a medium pan. Heat gently while stirring, until the sugar dissolves. Bring to a boil and simmer very gently, uncovered, without stirring for 5 minutes.

3. Remove from the heat and stir in all the remaining ingredients. Spread into the prepared pan and chill. When set, drizzle over the melted white chocolate and cut into bars.

COOKIE TIP
To prevent the corn syrup from clinging to the side of the measuring cup, lightly grease the cup first or spray it with nonstick cooking spray.

TANGY CREAM CHEESE Bars

Cream cheese blends best if allowed to soften at room temperature for a good hour before mixing.

MAKES: 18
BAKING TIME: 25–30 MINUTES

INGREDIENTS
¾ cup/1½ sticks butter, softened
4 ounces full-fat cream cheese
¾ cup sugar
1 egg
2 tablespoons orange juice
2 tablespoons lemon juice
Scant ½ cup mixed candied peel
2⅓ cups all-purpose flour
1 teaspoon baking powder

FROSTING
Scant 1 cup confectioners' sugar
1 tablespoon orange or lemon juice

1. Preheat the oven to 375°F. Grease a shallow 9 x 9-inch square pan.

2. Beat the butter and cream cheese together, then add the sugar and continue to beat until pale and fluffy. Beat in the egg. Beat in the fruit juices and stir in the mixed candied peel.

3. Sift the flour and baking powder together and add to the mixture to form a soft dough. Roll out on a lightly floured counter to a square that will fit the bottom of the prepared pan. Place in pan.

4. Bake until golden, 25–30 minutes. Let cool in the pan.

5. Cut into bars. Sift the confectioners' sugar into a small bowl and stir in enough juice to make a smooth frosting. Drizzle the frosting over the bars and let set.

COOKIE TIP
Be sure to store these in the refrigerator as cream cheese is perishable.

GINGER OAT
Squares

A crisp base and a chewy ginger oat topping give these cookies a fabulous contrast of textures.

MAKES: 12
BAKING TIME: 25 MINUTES

INGREDIENTS

1¼ cups all-purpose flour
1 teaspoon ground ginger
½ cup/1 stick butter
¼ cup light brown sugar, firmly
   packed
1–2 tablespoons water

TOPPING

4 pieces preserved ginger in syrup
3 tablespoons preserved ginger syrup
¼ cup/½ stick butter
2 tablespoons light brown sugar,
   firmly packed
1 cup rolled oats

1. Preheat the oven to 375°F. Lightly grease a 9 x 9-inch square pan.

2. Place the flour and ground ginger in a mixing bowl and rub in the butter until the mixture resembles fine bread crumbs. Stir in the sugar. Add enough water to mix to a soft dough. Roll out and use to line the bottom of the pan.

3. To make the topping: chop the ginger. Place in a pan with the syrup, butter, and sugar. Heat gently, stirring until the butter melts and the mixture is well blended.

4. Stir in the oats. Spread the mixture evenly over the dough. Bake until golden brown, about 25 minutes. Let cool in the pan and cut into squares to serve.

APRICOT & ALMOND Slices

For a chewy, nutty flavor that is out of this world, you can't beat these fruit slices.

MAKES: 16
BAKING TIME: 20 MINUTES

INGREDIENTS
2 cups all-purpose flour
3 tablespoons confectioners' sugar
1 teaspoon baking powder
¾ cup/1½ sticks butter
2 egg yolks

TOPPING
Scant ¼ cup apricot jelly
2 egg whites
½ cup sugar
Scant ½ cup ground almonds
Scant ½ cup sliced almonds

GLAZE
¼ cup apricot jelly

1. Preheat the oven to 375°F. Lightly grease a 9 x 9-inch square baking pan.

2. Sift the flour, confectioners' sugar, and baking powder into a mixing bowl. Cut the butter into cubes and blend until the mixture resembles fine bread crumbs. Stir in the egg yolks. Using your fingertips, work the mixture together to form a smooth dough, adding a little cold water if necessary. Roll or press out the dough to fit the bottom of the prepared pan and prick all over with a fork. Bake until just golden, about 10 minutes. Remove from the oven.

3. To make the topping: spread the apricot jelly over the crust. Beat the egg whites until frothy but not stiff. Stir in the sugar and ground almonds. Spread over the jelly and sprinkle the sliced almonds on top. Return to the oven until golden brown, about 20 minutes. Let cool in the pan. Carefully remove the pastry from the pan.

4. To make the glaze: melt the apricot jelly with 1 tablespoon water and brush over the surface to glaze. Cut into triangles to serve.

FIG & CINNAMON
Slices

Delicious on their own these fig slices also make a great dessert served with vanilla ice cream.

MAKES: 24–30
BAKING TIME: 10 MINUTES

INGREDIENTS
$\frac{1}{2}$ cup/1 stick butter
$\frac{1}{4}$ cup light brown sugar
1 teaspoon ground cinnamon
$1\frac{1}{2}$ cups all-purpose flour
$2\frac{1}{2}$ cups dried figs
1 cinnamon stick
$\frac{1}{2}$ cup superfine sugar
Finely grated zest of 1 lemon

1. Preheat the oven to 350°F. Lightly grease and base line a $10\frac{1}{2}$ x 7-inch baking pan.

2. Beat together the butter, brown sugar, and cinnamon until creamy. Mix in the flour and then press the mixture evenly into the pan pressing down with the back of a spoon or your fingertips. Bake for 15 minutes until golden but not brown.

3. Meanwhile put the figs, cinnamon stick, sugar and $1\frac{1}{2}$ cups boiling water into a saucepan. Bring to a boil, stirring. Reduce the heat and simmer gently for 15 minutes until the figs have softened and water reduced by about a third.

4. Remove the cinnamon stick. Add the lemon zest. Process the mixture until smooth in a food processor.

5. Spread the fig puree over the cooked base and bake for 10 minutes until set. Cool in the pan. Cut into squares when cold.

COOKIE TIP
Only store one kind of cookie in a container. If you mix crisp and soft cookies they will all go soft and end up tasting the same.

HAZELNUT & CINNAMON Meringues

A soft slightly chewy meringue with a warm spicy flavor.

MAKES: 50
BAKING TIME: 45 MINUTES

INGREDIENTS
3 egg whites
¾ cup superfine sugar
½ cup ground hazelnuts
1 teaspoon ground cinnamon
9 ounces milk chocolate

COOKIE TIP

Alternatively, you can use ground almonds and use bittersweet chocolate instead of milk chocolate.

1. Preheat the oven to 250°F. Line baking sheets with parchment paper.

2. Put the egg whites into a bowl and beat with a hand-held electric beater until the mixture stands in soft peaks. Beat in the sugar a little at a time, beating well between each addition. Fold in the nuts and cinnamon.

3. Put the mixture into a pastry bag fitted with a large plain tip. Pipe in 2-inch rounds on the prepared baking sheets. Flatten the tops with a wetted spatula.

4. Bake in the oven for about 45 minutes until dry to the touch. Turn the oven off leaving the meringues in the oven to dry out.

5. Melt the chocolate in the microwave or in a bowl over a pan of hot water. Either half dip the meringues in the chocolate or just coat the edges. Leave to set on parchment paper.

CITRUS
Squares

These fruity squares pack a real citrus punch to perk up your afternoon.

MAKES: 15
BAKING TIME: 32–40 MINUTES

INGREDIENTS
1¹⁄₈ cups all-purpose flour
¹⁄₃ cup confectioners' sugar
Scant ¹⁄₂ cup unsalted butter
TOPPING
2 eggs
³⁄₄ cup golden superfine sugar
Finely grated zest of lemon
Finely grated zest of 1 small orange
4 tablespoons lime juice
1 tablespoon all-purpose flour
¹⁄₂ teaspoon baking soda

1. Preheat the oven to 350°F. Grease and base line a 10¹⁄₂ x 7¹⁄₂-inch shallow baking pan.

2. Put the flour, confectioners' sugar, and butter into a food processor. Using the pulse button, process until the mixture comes together to make a firm dough. Press the dough evenly into the prepared pan and bake for 12–15 minutes until golden but not brown.

3. Beat the eggs until frothy. Gradually beat in the sugar and continue until the mixture is thick and foamy. Beat in the lemon and orange zest and lime juice. Beat in the flour and baking soda. Pour over the baked base. Bake for 20–25 minutes until golden brown.

4. Cool in the pan and then cut into squares.

COOKIE TIP
If a recipe calls for both lemon zest and juice, pour the lemon juice over the zest to keep it moist.

NO-BAKE CHOCOLATE FUDGE Bars

The beauty of these bars is their simplicity— and their unadulterated chocolate hit!

MAKES: 12

INGREDIENTS

8 ounces vanilla wafers

½ cup/1 stick butter

2 tablespoons light corn syrup

2 tablespoons unsweetened cocoa powder

4 ounces milk chocolate, broken into pieces

3 tablespoons confectioners' sugar

2 tablespoons milk

1. Lightly grease an 8 x 8-inch square pan. Place the wafers in a plastic bag and crush to produce fine crumbs with a rolling pin. Alternatively, process the wafers to crumbs in a food processor.

2. Place the butter, corn syrup, and cocoa in a small pan and heat gently until melted and blended, while stirring. Add the crumbs and stir until well combined.

3. Press the mixture into the pan and let chill until firm, at least 1 hour.

4. Melt the chocolate together with the confectioners' sugar and milk in a small bowl over a pan of hot water. Spread over the crumb crust and let set before cutting into bars.

COOKIE TIP
Most confectioners' sugar, also known as powdered sugar, is blended with a small amount of cornstarch to prevent major lumping. Even so, it's usually best to sift it prior to use.

PEPPERMINT CHOC Sticks

These cookies are deceptively easy to make and are absolutely delicious served with coffee at the end of a meal.

MAKES: 12–15

INGREDIENTS

9 ounces bittersweet chocolate

2 ounces clear hard peppermints, crushed

5 ounces Amaretti cookies, crushed

1. Melt the chocolate in a heatproof bowl over a pan of simmering water.

2. Remove from the heat and allow to cool slightly. Stir in the remaining ingredients.

3. Place a 12 x 4-inch sheet of parchment paper on a baking sheet. Spread the mixture evenly over the paper leaving a narrow edge. Let set.

4. When firm use a saw edge knife and carefully cut into thin sticks.

COOKIE TIP

Because this is such an easy recipe to make, it gives you more time to be creative with the shape of the cookie. Instead of sticks the mixture can be spread out and cut into thin squares or disks.

INDEX

RECIPE CREDITS

JACQUELINE BELLEFONTAINE

Pages 20, 21, 24, 25, 26 ,27, 28, 29, 32, 34, 35, 39, 44, 45, 48, 49, 50, 51, 54, 55, 56, 57, 58, 59, 62, 70, 71, 74, 75, 78, 69, 82, 83, 84, 86, 88, 94, 99, 120, 122, 123, 124, 125, 126, 128, 129, 130, 131, 132, 139, 144, 145, 146, 147, 150, 151, 154, 155, 159, 166, 168, 172, 173, 176, 177, 178, 183

VALERIE BARRETT

Pages 22, 30, 33, 36, 38, 40, 52, 60, 63, 66, 72, 76, 80, 89, 90, 96, 100, 101, 102, 104, 106, 107, 108, 110, 112, 114, 115, 116, 134, 136, 137, 138, 152, 156, 158, 160, 162, 163, 169, 170, 174, 179, 180, 182, 184

LORNA BRASH

Pages 95, 98, 105, 111

JENNY WHITE

Pages 87, 140, 148

MAGGIE MAYHEW

Pages 64, 65, 133

PHOTOGRAPHY CREDITS

MARIE LOUISE AVERY

Pages 2, 7 top, 8, 9, 10, 11, 13, 14, 16 left, 17, 18–19, 22, 31, 36, 42–43, 47, 52, 61, 63, 66, 68–69, 73, 77, 81, 85, 91, 92–93, 97, 103, 109, 113, 117, 118–119, 121, 127, 135, 141, 142–143, 149, 152, 157, 161, 164–165, 171, 175, 181, 185

CHRIS ALACK

Pages 3, 5, 6, 7 bottom, 15, 20, 24, 29, 32, 34, 35, 39, 49, 50, 55, 56, 58, 59, 62, 64, 70, 78, 86, 88, 94, 95, 98, 105, 111, 122, 125, 129, 130, 132, 139, 145, 147, 151, 154, 155, 159, 167, 169, 172, 173, 177, 178,